HEAVENLY HURTS
Surviving AIDS-Related
Deaths and Losses

HEAVENLY HURTS
Surviving AIDS-Related
Deaths and Losses

Sandra Jacoby Klein

Death, Value and Meaning Series
Series Editor: John D. Morgan

Baywood Publishing Company, Inc.
AMITYVILLE, NEW YORK

Cover photo by Neil Klein

Library of Congress Catalog Number: 97-20522
ISBN: 0-89503-181-7 (Cloth)

Library of Congress Cataloging-in-Publication Data

Klein, Sandra Jacoby.
    Heavenly hurts : surviving AIDS-related deaths and losses / Sandra Jacoby Klein.
        p.   cm. - - (Death, value and meaning series)
    Includes bibliographical references and index.
    ISBN 0-89503-181-7 (cloth)
    1. AIDS (Disease)- -Psychological aspects.   2. AIDS (Disease)-
-Patients- -Death.   3. Bereavement.   I. Title.   II. Series.
RC607.A26K5753 1998
362.1'969792'0019- -dc21   97-20522
                                                               CIP

Preface

This book is written because of the encouragement I have received, and continue to receive, from patients, friends, and colleagues with whom I have ongoing discussions about the grief surrounding death from AIDS-related illnesses. I have presented case histories, ideas, and theories at International Conferences on AIDS and at those on Grief and Bereavement. I continue to provide in-service training and support to clients and staff at AIDS service organizations. A co-therapist, Bill Fletcher, LCSW, and I led grief support groups for survivors of deaths from AIDS-related illnesses for many years. From each of my presentations, people request "something in writing" so they will have guidelines for dealing with the devastation of this disease. Caregivers who provide support, resources, and education to bereaved persons may also be trying to cope with their own grief from AIDS-related losses. Hopefully, professional and non-professional caregivers who search for information will read my book and find additional alternatives to the skills they currently find effective.

HIV/AIDS involves multiple losses including, but not limited to deaths. The needs of survivors experiencing these multiple losses often get ignored or minimized. Some mourners and helpers may be dealing with their first loss related to AIDS. Others, such as employees of AIDS service organizations or members of a community devastated by AIDS, are dealing with so many losses that they may not have the time to process their grief. I am offering information to help (1) *enhance coping skills;* (2) *understand the value of support systems;* (3) *use community resources;* and (4) *gain an awareness of the issues faced by all who are affected by HIV/AIDS.*

**This book is written for any or all of
the following readers:**

- **Any person grieving the death of someone from AIDS.**
- **Persons living with HIV/AIDS.**
- **Family members, friends, and co-workers of Persons Living with HIV/AIDS.**
- **Professional caregivers such as doctors, nurses, and hospital or hospice workers** wanting to increase their awareness of survivor issues.
- **Mental health counselors** to enhance their sensitivity to the needs of the survivors of AIDS-related deaths and losses.
- **AIDS service organizations' employees** to enhance their capacity to sustain themselves, their agency volunteers and co-workers, and to better serve their clients, client's significant others, and the community at large.
- **Employers and employees** dealing with deaths from AIDS-related illnesses.

The term professional caregiver is defined as anyone "who supplies resources to those undergoing a loss—therapists and counselors, physicians, nurses, clergy, social workers, hospice volunteers, funeral directors—anyone working with those who have suffered a loss of any kind" [1]. Non-professional caregivers or anyone else involved in some way with the person living with AIDS (PLWA) usually include spouses, partners, friends, family members (either biological or chosen), neighbors, and co-workers.

The populations hardest hit by HIV/AIDS have received the greatest support from within their own communities. Subsequently, those who are caregivers are frequently also the mourners. Gay and lesbian therapists, for example, may be supportive as professionals but are also members of the community in need of support themselves. Friends and family members may have experienced multiple losses but may lack specific information regarding the disease or the grief process.

The concerns and interests of professionals who are survivors may be different from those of mourners who are lay persons. Knowing this can help all caregivers work together with respect for their unique roles.

As a Marriage and Family Therapist, I specialize in the emotional effects of illness and grief. I am frequently asked, "How can you do this depressing work?" My answer: Affirming life never ends. It is rewarding and gratifying to give people tools and support to help them deal with their anxieties, fears, multiple losses, and deaths of loved ones. Helping the bereaved to mourn, survive, move on, and integrate death into life is one of my greatest challenges. It seemed natural to specialize in something I thought I knew well. I didn't realize at the time how much I would learn from those who came to work with me.

I have felt humbled many times during the course of my career as a psychotherapist/family therapist. Having "death and dying" as a specialty creates many 'down times' but also many more 'up times' than I could ever have imagined. That anyone, near the obvious end of their life, would have the courage to take the time to explore their psyche, says volumes for the human spirit. That they would choose to spend precious time with me, humbles me.

REFERENCE

1. C. M. Sanders, *Grief: The Mourning After. Dealing with Adult Bereavement,* John Wiley & Sons, New York, 1989.

Acknowledgments

The love, acceptance, and pride from my parents, Nathan and Florence Jacoby; my husband, Donald McCallum; and my children, Janeen and Bill Fetterman, Andrea Klein, and Neil Klein, are motivating forces for me to be the best I can be. I am deeply grateful for my family and friends, and for my patients. All of who give me more than I could ever repay with words.

From the bottom of my heart, I thank the following people to let them know how much I appreciate their interest and time spent reading the drafts and offering suggestions and encouragements, all of which enhanced this book. Thank you, thank you: Al Saunders, brother-in-law with wisdom and expert advice; John Morgan, Ph.D., my editor, enthusiastic and supportive; Linda Levinson, LCSW, tireless and patient reader and friend; Nancy Mattoon, MLS, librarian extraordinaire; and Judy Stone, MA, artist, teacher, and friend. To Rabbi Denise Eger, Kathy Jackson, Ph.D., Barbara and Marc Bresler, and Michelle and Steven Windmueller, many thanks for your continuous encouragement, support, and friendship.

I am deeply indebted to my teachers and colleagues in the often unpopular and misunderstood field of thanatology. My ideas, the terminology I use, and my faith in the work I do, have been developed and encouraged over the years by access to their teachings, writings, and presentations. I hope those colleagues who read this book will recognize their words and ideas and know that I try to use them wisely.

Table of Contents

Introduction

Mark Katz, M.D. *

The HIV pandemic, well into its second decade and having claimed several hundreds of thousands of American lives, challenges our society with a plethora of issues—from research questions (many of them unanswered) to health care resource allocation to political activism to a psychosocial burden almost beyond comprehension.

High among these issues is that of loss, the fundamental issue of this loss usually being multiple. "How can we stop mourning when the next death has already descended?" spoke an activist from the hard-hit San Francisco gay community several years ago.

There are few to no road maps available for directing people toward answers to such salient issues as:

How is AIDS grief similar to, and different from, that of cancer and other life-terminating illnesses?

How does one deal with the notion that many of the mourners are themselves infected and may be preparing for their own deaths?

*Mark Katz, M.D. has presented over 100 monthly HIV/AIDS Medical Updates in the Los Angeles, California area under the auspices of Being Alive. This is an organization of and for people living with HIV and AIDS. He is an Emergency Room physician for Kaiser Permanente in Southern California.

How can a community offer support when the community itself is decimated by the same disease?

Can support be effectively given when the caregivers are themselves dealing with private loss issues (from, again, the same underlying condition)?

To what extent does the stigmatization attached to HIV/AIDS create a barrier to either the giving or the receiving of such?

How does one deal with the guilt of survivors who have remained uninfected, when many have had the same lifestyle risks as those whom they are grieving?

How do different cultures handle the burden of AIDS loss, and can caregivers be taught to be culturally appropriate?

This list can go on and on, for AIDS, indeed, is a global challenge of the end of the twentieth century (one which will most likely endure well into the first years of the twenty-first!). As medical science fosters improvements in survival, persons with HIV live to develop conditions which were practically unheard of during the epidemic's early years.

The need has been great for several years for a manuscript which would help support caregivers as well as mourners as they deal with the (usually multiple) loss which is attached to AIDS. What lies ahead in the pages to follow is a superb tome which looks at answers to all of the above questions, and more.

Sandra Jacoby Klein has been a pillar of wisdom, support, and strength in the affected community of Los Angeles since the beginning of the epidemic. As a physician, I have often called on her because of her unique blend of style (compassionate and loving) and substance (experienced and insightful). I am grateful that her work has been realized in written form, encapsulating more than fifteen years of her experience. This book can be used by persons directly impacted by HIV, as well as their caregivers, loved ones, and co-workers.

She is comfortable talking about "the language of death," and in this book helps impart such to the reader. Her chapter on "Dealing with Death in the Workplace," is unique and thoughtful, and indeed must be read! Her comparisons of AIDS losses versus disease losses, or AIDS-related grief versus clinical depression, may ultimately serve as the standards for many therapists.

Ms. Jacoby Klein's work has been presented internationally, and her reputation is solid as the pre-eminent expert in AIDS multiple loss. Having this newly compiled book that is filled with insight and caring, creates a pool of relief in the vast sea of HIV/AIDS. Read on, imbibe, and reflect. I hope you can soon be feeling some of the appreciation which I, and many others, feel for all she has done!

There's a certain Slant of Light
Winter Afternoons—
That oppresses, like the Heft
Of Cathedral Tunes—

Heavenly Hurt it gives us—
We can find no scar,
But internal difference,
Where the Meanings, are—

None may teach it—Any—
'Tis the Seal Despair—
An imperial affliction
Sent us of the Air—

When it comes, the Landscape listens—
Shadows—hold their breath—
When it goes, 'tis like the Distance
On the look of Death—

Emily Dickinson

CHAPTER 1

Understanding HIV and AIDS

People still have a hard time accepting that
HIV is an equal opportunity virus.

What is AIDS? AIDS, or acquired immune deficiency syndrome, is a disease caused by the human immune deficiency virus (HIV) that destroys the body's natural ability to fight illness. Diseases such as pneumonia and rare cancers develop as the virus causes a breakdown in the body's immune system. One or more of these diseases actually cause death. AIDS has an impact on people of all races, cultures, and ethnic groups.

As of June 1996, the estimated prevalence of persons living with AIDS was 223,000 U.S. residents. The World Health Organization estimates over 750,000 persons live with HIV/AIDS in North America alone which accounts for only 3.7 percent of the total number of persons living with HIV/AIDS worldwide [1]. The numbers of those infected with HIV will be larger than the numbers of AIDS cases simply because being infected doesn't mean one has AIDS. HIV is an infectious disease. An infected person appearing to be in good health is contagious and can transmit the virus. Anyone with either HIV or AIDS is able to transmit the virus to others. HIV is contagious only when passed from an infected person by way of bodily fluids such as: blood, semen, or vaginal secretions. It is not a virus contracted by casual contact such as shaking hands, kissing, touching the deceased, or picked up from a toilet seat.

It is believed that 8,000 people a day are newly infected with HIV. People become infected with this very dynamic HIV in a variety of ways. The most common way is through unprotected sexual contact that allows the exchange of bodily fluids between an infected person and an uninfected person, homosexual or heterosexual. The virus is also spread through the shared use of syringes during the injection of drugs. The uninfected person receives infected blood from the needle and syringe. An infected pregnant woman can transmit the virus to her fetus during birth. An infected mother can infect her child through her breast milk. Many people also became infected through blood transfusions at a time when the blood supply was not screened for HIV antibodies. (The test which does so was not licensed until 1985.) Some health care workers have been infected by accidental needle sticks.

The period of time between infection and the development of AIDS can be longer than ten years. A person is given a diagnosis of AIDS after he or she develops one of the opportunistic diseases associated with this virus. Much is known about AIDS since its discovery in the early 1980s but even as knowledge increases and newer medications offer hope, AIDS still has no cure or vaccine.

Who has AIDS? According to the *Morbidity and Mortality Weekly Report,* from 1981 through 1996, a total of 573,800 adult persons with AIDS were reported to the Centers for Disease Control (CDC) [2]. From 1992 through 1996, non-Hispanic blacks, Hispanics, and women accounted for increasing proportions of persons reported with AIDS with women accounting for an all-time high of 20 percent of adults.

The CDC has documented over 5.8 million deaths due to AIDS-related illness since the early 1980s. Approximately 49,600 persons died in 1994 and approximately 50,000 died in 1995. During January to June 1996, deaths began to decline with 22,000 dying during this six-month period. Despite the trend toward decrease in deaths, during 1995, complications of HIV infection remained the leading cause of death among persons aged twenty-five to forty-four years. The decrease in AIDS deaths reflects the increased survival among persons with AIDS due to improvements in medical care, development of new medications, and the use of combination drugs to treat opportunistic infections as well as the underlying virus.

As noted, the worldwide demographic profile of the HIV-infected population is changing, with gay men no longer the largest infected population. However, in the United States, gay men have disproportionately experienced the greatest number of deaths (often hundreds of friends) and other losses. They have developed coping skills to deal with their experiences. What we have learned from the way these men are handling multiple losses can be a model for other populations who are now facing the same issues of infection, illness, and death.

AIDS has been called "the Great Disenfranchiser" [3]. When a death is due to an AIDS-related illness, it creates a great challenge for the survivors because of a deep fear attached to this disease. Society has not found a way to dispel the myths or get rid of the stigma and judgments attached to the diverse population infected by this virus. People are at times appropriately afraid to tell the truth to family, friends, and their employers for fear of discrimination, ridicule, rejection, and physical violence. Unfortunately it may take the widespread infection of thousands more before society drops the stigma of HIV/AIDS and offers compassionate care to all.

Unfortunately, the mode of transmission has become a pawn in the mistreatment of those who are infected. There is a recognized hierarchy of "acceptable" ways of becoming infected as opposed to the accusation leveled at the gay community of, "You brought it on yourself." Infected babies or those infected through transfusions with "bad blood" are often called innocent victims. Other adults who contract the disease are seen as self-indulgent and irresponsible, viewed with disdain and seen as not being deserving of support. As people live longer with HIV due to continuing advances in treatments and medications, AIDS can become more like a chronic illness instead of one with a series of acute episodes. For the duration of the infection, the person is living, not only with the disease, but also with the stigma attached to it.

It may be called a chronic but not life-threatening illness, but that doesn't mean it is any less easy to manage. The often debilitating infections and their after-effects remain. People are still suffering from neurological damage, caused by medications and/or the disease process, that limits their mobility. The purpose of treatment is to decrease the viral load, slow its progression through the body, preserve immune function, and prolong survival. Those who can afford the high cost of new drugs to accomplish the above steps, must take multiple medications that require coordination with meals. Patients often limit certain activities, like vacations, in order to remain close to their doctors. In a tongue-in-cheek article in an AIDS Project Los Angeles publication, Paul Serchia who is living with AIDS, writes, "The CDC announced today that the condition formerly known as AIDS has been reclassified as manageable acquired immune deficiency syndrome. So currently in the United States, there are over 550,000 people with MAIDS" [4, p. 4].

If the treatment fails and the disease progresses, most people with AIDS become quite ill for an extended period of time before they die. With the progression of the disease comes the need for labor-intensive caregiving. The professional caregivers such as doctors, nurses, therapists, and case workers count in the hundreds the patients they cared for who have died. They rarely have time to grieve an individual's death before more gravely ill patients come along. The number of people involved with and caring for these patients will continue to increase. People close to a person with AIDS, who take on the role of caregiver, experience demands on their time as well, by having to change the priorities of their daily life. At the same time, they are dealing with the potential loss of a significant person in their life.

When death occurs, the survivors are impacted in many ways by the loss of the deceased. The person who died might have been part of a committed gay couple, or a single parent with surviving children who need to be cared for by others. The newly deceased may have been the surviving spouse of a couple where both have now died of AIDS-related illness. It is possible that a family could be decimated, with both parents and one or more children dead of this disease. There have been cases where infected children have died before their infected parents. It goes on and on with any combination of deaths that we can think of.

Children and adolescents who are survivors of AIDS deaths can be overwhelmed by the confusion of their feelings including fear, anger, grief, abandonment, and sadness. They may have to keep secrets about their parents' death to avoid discrimination from their teachers and peers, needing to decide whom they can trust before sharing the truth. These children not only have to deal with their grief; they also have to deal with judgments and reactions about how their parents died. Outside support is often needed, not only because of the stigma associated with HIV/AIDS, but also because surviving adult relatives are often overwhelmed by their own grief and anger.

People in many roles and relationships may define themselves as "survivors." These persons might include lovers, partners, siblings, friends, co-workers, employers and employees, parents and children, and grandparents and grandchildren. They will experience the grief and the consequences of grief that accompany surviving the death from AIDS of someone close.

Depending on the nature of the relationship, the survivor will experience some or all of the struggles discussed in this book. Thus, those helping survivors mourn, also need to help the survivors understand their grief. They can do this by encouraging an exploration of the survivor's relationship with the deceased. If a counselor does not ask questions about the mourner's relationship with the person who died, the counselor will not be aware of the specific and personal issues of each griever.

The diagnosis of multiple family members infected with HIV is another difficult situation encountered in this disease. The most frequent occurrence of this kind is due to injection drug use by multiple family members, engaging in unsafe sexual practices after infection, or transmission of HIV to a fetus. The deaths of multiple family members, in bits and pieces, can take place over a period of years as contrasted with multiple deaths that occur all at once due to an accident or natural disaster. Survivors in HIV/AIDS situations are often overwhelmed by the ongoing decimation and caregiving in the family as bereavement becomes a constant. Situations in an individual's life that were hidden before HIV/AIDS, cannot easily be kept secret any more. If survivors choose to attend support groups it is important for facilitators to understand their secrets, discomfort, and fears. The issues of HIV/AIDS including homosexuality, substance use, and multiple sex partners are confusing and it is helpful to determine how each of these issues is affecting the grief.

For purposes of clarity I have chosen to define some commonly used words related to HIV and AIDS (Public Health Service) [5]. Some are used throughout this book and others may be heard while speaking to surviving family members, friends, or caregiving professionals:

- *HIV-Positive*: Antibodies to HIV, when present in the blood, confirm HIV infection. Infection does not mean a person automatically has AIDS, or will develop AIDS.
- *HIV-Negative*: Not being infected with the HIV. No HIV antibodies found in the blood. This may mean that there has been no infection with HIV or it may mean that the person is in the "window period" where one is infected but antibodies have not yet developed.
- *Immune System*: A complex network of specialized organs and cells that has evolved to defend the body against potential infections.
- *Immune-Suppression*: Suppression of the immune system's response by drugs, disease, or radiation that lowers the body's resistance to disease. A person with AIDS thus develops a variety of life-threatening illnesses.
- *Helper T-Cells*: One of the body's defenses to fight off viruses. These cells turn on antibody production.
- *T-Cell Count*: Reduction of these cells (specifically, the T-helper or T-4 or CD4 proportion) occurs after infection with HIV. Tracking the numbers is one way doctors monitor the course of the disease.
- *Viral Load*: Indicates how much of the HIV is in the body. The Viral Load Test tells how fast the virus is damaging the immune system.
- *Seroconversion*: When infection with HIV causes a previously HIV-Negative person to become HIV-Positive.
- *Opportunistic Infections*: Infections that are likely to occur when the immune system is weak. Organisms that do not affect people whose immune systems are working normally,

cause these infections. Included are Pneumocystis pneumonia, Kaposi's sarcoma (a cancer-like illness, recently discovered to be associated with a newly identified virus, producing purplish lesions on the skin. Can also be found internally), Candidiasis (yeast infections), CMV retinitis and Non-Hodgkins lymphoma (a malignancy of the lymph glands).

- *Protease Inhibitors*: Powerful medications, first licensed by the FDA in late 1995 which have the ability to significantly reduce the level of detectable HIV in the blood.
- *PLWA*: person living with AIDS.
- *Homophobic*: Behavior or act based upon having an aversion to homosexual people, their behavior, or their culture.
- *Syndrome*: A group of symptoms that collectively characterize a disease or abnormal condition.
- *Epidemic*: Outbreak of a disease that is rare in a community, but which suddenly spreads rapidly to affect a large number of people.
- *Pandemic*: Widespread epidemic worldwide proportions.

The importance of terminology is to help supply answers to the frequent questions of caregivers dealing with HIV/AIDS. They ask, "What are the issues?" "What are the words to use to talk about this illness?" and "What does it mean to use them?" "Is there a difference between using them with those who are knowledgeable about HIV/AIDS than there is using them with friends who have not experienced AIDS grief?" "What is it like to use the words in conversations with those who are unfamiliar with AIDS grief?" "Does mutual understanding of issues and phrases increase isolation or increase connection?"

AIDS is forcing society to recognize and acknowledge the diversity of sexual orientations. Opening dialogues and communicating differences is healthy, but it also seems to bring out fear, shame, disgust and hatred, all of which are divisive and will contribute to continued ostracism of infected and affected persons. Ultimately, no matter what our sexual orientation, we all have the potential to become infected with HIV.

Each of us might someday be touched by AIDS. We may all know someone who has become infected with HIV. AIDS has the potential to surpass the polio epidemic of the late twentieth century and eradication will only happen if we continue to stress the importance of personal responsibility and community awareness. To accomplish this end we need ongoing effective education and prevention programs and increased funding for research.

UNDERSTANDING HIV/AIDS

- Caregivers and survivors have issues that need to be understood, respected, and supported.

- AIDS has its own terminology and knowing AIDS language helps people communicate more clearly and feel less alone.

- It is helpful to know the level of familiarity someone has with HIV/AIDS when seeking their support and understanding.

- It is normal to both want to run away and want to be the ultimate caregiver when faced with caring for and comforting someone with HIV/AIDS.

REFERENCES

1. World Health Organization, *Weekly Epidemiological Record,* Geneva, Switzerland, July 5, 1996.
2. Centers for Disease Control, *Morbidity and Mortality Weekly Report, 46*:8, Update: Trends in AIDS Incidence, Deaths, and Prevalence—United States, 1996, Atlanta, Georgia, 1997.
3. K. Doka, *Disenfranchised Grief: Recognizing Hidden Sorrow,* Lexington Books, Lexington, Massachusetts, 1989.
4. P. Serchia, *Positive Living,* AIDS Project Los Angeles, November 1996.
5. Public Health Service, Understanding the Immune System. U.S. Department of Health and Human Services, National Institutes of Health, *NIH Publication No. 85-529,* Bethesda, Maryland, 1985.

CHAPTER 2

Understanding Death, Loss, and Feelings of Grief

Dying is not a neurosis. Individuals dealing with multiple deaths due to AIDS are likely to lose sight of this fact as they struggle with grieving one death after another. Dying is something that happens to all of us at some point in time. It is a natural and normal part of living that happens to be something that isn't popular to acknowledge, talk about, or plan for. Mostly, all people hope they will live to a ripe old age with all their faculties intact and then just die quickly and quietly. When asked, people tend to be more afraid of the dying process than they are of death itself. Because of this fear, people often say that they want to die in their sleep without any suffering. Unfortunately, the way a person dies is not usually in his or her control. The inevitability of death, therefore, cannot be altered, but our attitudes toward death can change.

Even though people tend to think in terms of death as a loss, death is not the *only* loss we can experience. Each of us has lived through many different kinds of loss—from moving from our home, changing our job, losing a wallet with all our credit cards, or having a pet die, to the very powerful impact of the death of a beloved person. Knowing that loss occurs in many forms makes us aware that loss touches us frequently as we go through our lives. Although each person's loss is unique and meaningful, the feelings associated with grief, (anger, emptiness, fear, frustration, guilt, searching, and physical discomfort), are common to all of us and normal grief covers a broad range of feelings, physical sensations, cognitions, and behaviors [1].

Loss and separation can also occur at many levels. For example, when a child starts school the separation from mother and home can be quite traumatic. If the family moves there is a separation from the community and a loss of friends and familiar places. If a couple makes a mutual decision to separate, and they subsequently divorce, both feel the loss, as do their children (if any) and other family members and friends. If lovers decide to go their separate ways, they have to face fears and conquer them as they re-enter a dating society and move forward to make new friends as individuals instead of as a couple.

Reaching a desired goal of weight loss, organizing closets by giving away or getting rid of clothes no longer worn, finishing an absorbing book or project, are all positive goals. At the same time, these activities involve loss. Losses cause an upset in our equilibrium even when seen as positive and desirable. Endings, and/or changes of any kind involve loss, and can result in transitory feelings of grief that, when processed, enable people to regain a sure footing and then continue with their life. Death is certainly the most profound of all endings and the most stressful. It is so final and out of one's control. No matter how expected it may be, it always catches one off guard. Rarely is anyone ready for its finality.

When we talk about death and dying there seems to be a new vocabulary of grief words to learn. Words like loss, grief, mourning, and bereavement are often used interchangeably, but do they mean the same thing? Does it really matter which words are used or when they are spoken? Also, each culture may impart different meanings to similar words. Here are some definitions from the current literature on grief and bereavement:

Death: The act of dying. Irrevocable. Termination or end of life and cessation of vital activities.

Loss: Deprivation, act or an instance of losing something with a physical or emotional attachment. Condition of being deprived or bereaved of something or someone. Often there is secondary loss that comes as a consequence of the initial loss, e.g., having to move after the death of a spouse due to economic changes.

Bereavement: The state of having lost an object or person to which one had a bond.

Grief: The personal feelings and emotional reactions to loss. Grief is experienced psychologically, physically, behaviorally, and socially. It is a natural reaction to all types of loss, not just death, and involves many changes over time. It is very personal and individual.

Bereft: To have something taken while it still has value and meaning.

Mourn: To feel or express grief or sorrow. To make a low, indistinct, mournful sound. To show grief for a death by conventional signs. To feel or express deep regret for. To grieve over. To utter sorrowfully.

Mourning: Sorrowing, lamenting, grieving. Actions or expressions of one who is feeling bereft. The period during which a death is mourned and a person begins the process of healing and re-engaging with the world of the living. How one adapts to the loss of a loved one. Conscious and unconscious process of grief work.

In mourning the death of any loved one, a mixture of both physical and psychosocial losses, as well as a number of secondary losses, accrues. These secondary losses can be physical or psychosocial in nature and generate their own grief and mourning reactions. Because the death of a loved one brings many losses, what one perceives as a given individual's grief and mourning for a specific death is actually the sum total of all the grief and mourning for each of the losses experienced in connection with this death [2, p. 22].

Loss is complicated, and becoming familiar with the definitions of words related to this experience can help increase the understanding of the process of grief. This process is not linear, moving from the immediate period of the death to some kind of resolution. In fact, mourners move through their period of grief by alternately confronting and avoiding the grief. People have a common perception that there is a "normal" way to experience grief. In reality, there is great diversity in the way people mourn. Acknowledging this diversity means that it may become easier to incorporate death into life.

There is a spectrum of grief experiences that is sometimes viewed along gender lines in relation to AIDS deaths. Thoughts and feelings about the deceased tend to range from loving, overprotective, forgiving, and accepting to responses that are unemotional, withdrawn, and stoic. Partners may become angry with one another when they do not express grief in similar ways. Some may have difficulty accepting the possible cause of an AIDS death, and others may need to idolize the deceased. If support is to be meaningful to the survivor, each situation must be evaluated without judgment.

A person who is grieving may exhibit outward signs of grief by wearing a particular color or type of garment. For example, black clothes are often worn for an extended period of time. These customs serve a dual purpose. They announce to the world that the person is a mourner. They also keep the grieving person connected to the person who has died. Dressing in black everyday, a symbol of grief, reminds the survivor that the deceased really existed and mattered in life. Somber colors show that it is not the time to express joy. The wearing of black may even go against the wishes of the deceased, but the survivor feels compelled to continue the practice until ready to let go.

Marianna's family kept telling her that it was almost a year since her husband died of his AIDS-related illnesses and she could stop wearing black all the time. They reminded her that Dave told her not to wear dark clothes when he died. She was unable to change and said, "I know he hated me in black and loved me in colors and wanted me to remember that, but I just can't. I want the world to know what a horrible loss I've endured. If I take off the black clothes than I might not think of him everyday. I think it is a sign of respect. It just isn't time yet."

Thanatologists (those who study death) have described the grief process in different ways. The five stages by which the dying come to terms with their impending death have been described by Elisabeth Kübler-Ross: (1) Denial and isolation, (2) Anger, (3) Bargaining, (4) Depression, and (5) Acceptance [3, p. 28]. These stages have also defined common phases of grief for mourners. J. William Worden talks about the four tasks of mourning: (1) To accept the reality of the loss, (2) To experience the pain of grief, (3) To adjust to an environment in which the deceased is missing, and (4) To find an appropriate place for the person who died in the emotional life of the bereaved [1]. Alan Wolfelt describes tasks of mourning as reconciliation needs and identifies five: (1) To experience and express outside oneself the reality of the death; (2) To tolerate the emotional suffering that is inherent in the work of grief while nurturing oneself both physically and emotionally; (3) To convert the relationship with the deceased from one of presence to a relationship of memory; (4) To develop a new self-identity based on a life without the deceased; and (5) To relate the experience of loss to a context of meaning [4].

All agree that when a person is mourning it is normal to feel some or all of the following *responses to grief:*

Emotional release such as crying or screaming,
Utter depression, sense of isolation, deep sorrow,
Physical symptoms of distress such as illness or exhaustion,
Panic, self-doubt, and confusion,
Guilt feelings,
Hostility, anger, and rage,
Telling and retelling stories of a loved one and the death experience,
Inability to return to former activities,
Questioning the purpose of life,
Reevaluating goals and values,
Gradually overcoming grief feelings, and
Restitution, readjustment to life with, and without the deceased.

Some mourners feel less "crazy" knowing that there are words to describe emotions related to grief and that other people who grieve also feel these feelings. When mourners are unable to express themselves clearly, it is important to give them descriptive words for their confusion, intense feelings, and thoughts. Given the option to choose the words that most closely match how they feel at any given time, most mourners find that they are able to talk about their grief in a more meaningful way.

Using accurate words enables them to be clearer about their pain and more easily allows the listener to accept and understand them. Here are some common grief feelings and grief reactions:

Common Grief Feelings:

Depression	Fear	Anxiety
Irritability	Apathy	Feelings of unreality
Self-reproach	Guilt	Confusion
Numbness	Anger	Shock
Self-doubt	Panic	Deep sorrow

Common Grief Reactions:

Difficulty accepting loss	Painful yearning and longing
Constant tearfulness	Lack of meaning in life
Sense of losing one's mind	Inability to concentrate
Insomnia	Blaming others
Denial and disbelief	Social withdrawal
Change in sexual desire	Wanting to run away
Increased dreaming of the deceased	
Re-experiencing feelings related to previous deaths	
Assuming traits of the deceased	
Restlessness, aimless wandering	
Sense of being in the presence of the deceased	
Expecting the person to appear	

Most mourners will have *physical reactions* such as:

Sighing	Tightness in the throat
Trouble catching one's breath	
Loss of appetite	Weight loss
Heaviness in the chest	Exhaustion

Many themes run through the process of grief including those illustrated by the following anecdotes:

Even with so many descriptive words, a client shared that he didn't think "that just a list of adjectives would help anyone totally understand the depths of pain that multiple loss plays upon an individual." Many grieving persons undoubtedly think similar thoughts. A large part of the grief process is believing that "my pain is unique." To some extent, each person's loss is unique because one's relationship with the person who died was unlike any other relationship. Experiencing such uniqueness makes one wonder how anyone else could experience the intensity of emotions in a similar way.

It is difficult to imagine surviving the constant barrage and intensity of feelings of grief no matter what words one uses or actions one takes. It seems as though the pain will never lessen. Who among us has never felt the intense, confusing feelings associated with grief? Feelings like no others. The impact can double us over and make us question how we will survive. How will the emotional pain be managed? How can life possibly go on in the same ordinary way each day? The time after the death becomes a time of great perplexity. Survivors may feel shut down and closed off. They wonder if they are grieving enough or the "right way" even though they are unsure of what that might be.

James appeared totally distraught at a grief support group session. He related feeling terrible because of what had happened to him the previous evening. "I let some friends persuade me to go bowling with them even though it is only 5 months since Devon died. They practically had to drag me out of the house. They put on my bowling shoes over my protests and made me throw the ball. I almost went down the alley with it. Everybody started laughing and so did I. I started to have fun. I love to bowl. A couple of hours later I realized that I was having fun and started feeling so guilty, like I had let Devon down or forgotten him or something. It was awful."

The other group members listened to his story and several related having similar experiences. They also had similar feelings. As the members talked, they began to work through the intensity of the feelings of confusion and guilt. They realized how their grief had totally consumed them. Having fun offered respite time from the intensity of the grief. They were surprised and relieved to find that even while they were having fun, they had not stopped mourning their loved ones. The feelings are not mutually exclusive and can coexist for as long as needed.

Survivors question why they awaken each day feeling so displaced while everyone else seems to go on as usual. They wonder how others can be concerned with trivialities. The mourners become impatient with anyone who wants something from them no matter how simple the request. Everything feels intrusive. Most people in grief notice an increase in their feelings of intolerance. They complain of feeling irritable and angry most of the time.

The impact of his partner's death was so profound that Dale was shocked when the sun continued to rise each morning. He couldn't believe that the mundane aspects of daily life continued. "People are so concerned with trivial things. I can't believe that they are like this." He became impatient with any demand placed upon him. After expressing these thoughts and getting feedback and validation from the group members he began to accept that death coexists with life. Moving through each day and surviving a day at a time, can ultimately lead to a return to one's previous existence. This transition will occur even though one's life is forever changed.

Sometimes people want to join the loved one who died and think of what it might be like if they were to commit suicide. When Marian described the pain of her grief and the desire to join her father who had just died of AIDS-related illness, I first asked her if she had made a plan to kill herself. She replied, "I have saved all the pain pills my Dad had before he died. I know that people sometimes do this and take all the pills but they aren't enough to kill them. I don't want to be a vegetable. I want to die." I could hear the desperateness in her voice. I asked her if she would be willing to talk to her Dad about wanting to join him. She agreed to try. She told him how much she missed him and how angry she was that he died, especially of AIDS because she had to keep it a secret so her friends would still come near her. She said that she needed his advice regarding her college classes and how to apply for a student loan. She wanted him to give her away at her upcoming wedding and couldn't imagine getting married without him present. She spoke to him and sobbed in deep grief.

When she was able to compose herself, I asked her, "What do you think your Dad would say to you now?" She looked at me strangely and hesitated. Then she replied, "I think he would tell me that he is always with me in my heart. He understands my anger and says it would be good if I could find a way to talk about his death. He says that I know which classes I need and that the counselor will help with the loan money. He wanted to give me away and is really sorry that he can't be there in person but that I should carry something of his with me as I walk down the aisle." She paused and then said, "It is not OK that he died but I can see that I can make it without him. Mom and my fiancé would be devastated if I died also."

In follow-up sessions Marian told me that she had shared her suicidal thoughts with her mother and had reassured her that she was no longer thinking about killing herself. They were able to talk freely about their husband and father. Marian was bothered by questions about her Dad. She was able to ask her Mother and got answers and support. Her mother gave her a gold locket with a picture of her Dad that she could wear on her wedding day. Marian's fiancé received a ring that had belonged to her father. She continued to discuss her anger and grief in our sessions and going through the process of grief became healing for her.

Searching for reasons for the death of a loved one raises a million questions. People ask, "Were we to blame?" "Did we do too little?" "What more could we have done?" "There must have been something else!" Alice, a young friend of a deceased AIDS patient, attended one of our grief support group sessions. She asked all of the above questions and more. She reported that the unanswered questions filled her with guilt. Alice had not even been able to visit her dying friend. She said she could not handle seeing his debilitated condition and his body covered with the lesions of Kaposi's sarcoma (one of the opportunistic infections). Talking about this experience made her very emotional. Some of the members in attendance at the group that night had been devoted caregivers and shared their experiences. Several shared with her that they asked themselves the same questions.

They tried to reassure her that the illness was hard to deal with and that her avoidance was understandable. Even though the members of the group welcomed her and encouraged her to come back, she did not return. (We later found out that when she heard how dedicated the other caregivers were to their deceased partners it only made her feel more guilty.) Perhaps had she continued to express her feelings and thoughts in the group setting, she might have been able to let go of her anguish and guilt. The value of her friendship with the deceased man would have been validated and she would have been left with the good memories of their relationship.

Mourners often ask, "I am always sad and crying. Will I ever feel normal again?" Many survivors tell me that they don't want to cry because they are afraid that they will not be able to stop. They state, "I am afraid I might fall apart." I tell them that I will sit with them and they can cry as long as they want or need to shed tears for their loved one. If they want to cry at home, I suggest that they set a timer for a short period of time, say half an hour, and then just start feeling sad and let the tears flow. If they don't stop naturally, when the timer rings, they will stop. This is one way to convince the person that it is OK to cry. They will have control and they *will* be able to stop. Mourners can set limits and boundaries on the expression of their grief and it is healthier to cry in this manner than to withhold and internalize the tears.

More than one survivor has shared with me the belief that he or she was "going crazy." The thoughts and feelings of the experience of grief were so powerful, unusual and unrelated to anything previously experienced in their life. They became overwhelmed by their intense feelings and by their fears of losing control. Neil, a very responsible and organized accountant, forgot to pay his rent. He lost his car keys one day and then another day forgot where he parked his car. He was beside himself and said, "I don't recognize myself. What is going on? I can't concentrate and I think I am losing my mind." I explained that this behavior was a common, normal grief response. There was something he could do until this would pass and he was back to his old self. He felt reassured that there would be an old self to go back to! I suggested that he become extra vigilant and even make notes about things he would normally remember. I told him to carry a small notepad with him so he could jot down parking space numbers. He was advised to follow a routine for putting his keys and other belongings in place. These sounded like helpful suggestions for him and he was relieved to know that he was really OK.

Sometimes the mourners' own irrational behavior shocks them. Sam felt alone with his grief. At a gathering with his family no one mentioned his lover's recent death from AIDS. Finally in anger and a confusion of conflicting feelings, he ran out of the house and got into his car. He hurriedly backed down the driveway not caring that he nearly ran over his brother who was trying to stop him. Sam later became aware that he felt he had wanted to kill his brother for not paying attention to his grief and for being unsympathetic. He was consumed with remorse for acting and thinking like this.

He shared this story with his grief group one evening and the members helped him understand that the strong emotions he was directing toward his brother had to do with his frustrated need to express his grief to those closest to him. Eventually, he was able to tell his family that he needed to talk about the death. They believed that he would become upset if they started talking about Jerry so they avoided any discussion of his illness and death. Now the family surprised him by proving to be more supportive than he ever thought they would be.

It was helpful for grief group members to have an understanding of "stages" that people frequently go through during the mourning period. Many were familiar with Elisabeth Kübler-Ross' stages that were discussed earlier in this chapter. We were able to clarify for them that Kübler-Ross did not believe that people necessarily move through these stages in order. Kübler-Ross offered these stages as guidelines to help mourners name and understand the various feelings associated with the time of bereavement. Most tried to identify which stage they were in as it made them feel more "normal." James said, "I can't believe that Joseph died. I must be in the 'denial' stage. I feel better knowing there is a name for where I am." The group members learned that some mourners experience all of the stages, others only some of them. It became clear that there was no set order to the way they might go through these stages.

As mourners get in touch with and learn to express their feelings of grief, they are able to find some normalcy in their experience of grief. They not only share their feelings, but also hear from those who are surviving similar experiences. Mourners realize that their feelings are normal and appropriate. Eventually they will return to dealing with the mundane and the joyful aspects of daily life. Time can be set aside for grieving even as one goes about the activities of life. Finding a balance between death and life doesn't lessen the impact of the death or the meaning of the relationship. It does, however, allow the mourning activities to be placed into perspective.

UNDERSTANDING DEATH, LOSS, AND FEELINGS OF GRIEF

- A large part of the grief process is feeling and believing that each persons pain is unique and that the intensity will never lessen.

- There is no right way to grieve. Grief is expressed individually and mourners experience a wide range of thoughts and feelings.

- Grieving and having fun are not mutually exclusive.

- Normal grief reactions include feeling alone, angry, exhausted, easily frustrated with others. When feeling such pain, it is difficult to understand how people continue to go about their day-to-day activities.

- Mourners often feel it would be easier to die and join the deceased rather than deal with the pain of surviving the loss.

- Feeling the presence of the deceased may be confusing as it is often comforting and supportive.

- Survivors often feel anxious about whether they could have done more or if they were to blame for the death.

- The feelings of grief are so intense some people wonder if they are "going crazy." Many hold back tears for fear of not being able to stop crying once they let go.

- Being aware of the phases of grief can help survivors understand and accept the feelings they are experiencing.

- Participating in a support group for survivors of those who have died of AIDS-related illnesses can help answer questions, normalize reactions, and help participants feel more understood and less alone.

REFERENCES

1. J. W. Worden, *Grief Counseling and Grief Therapy,* Springer Publishing Company, Inc., New York, 1991.
2. T. Rando, *Treatment of Complicated Mourning,* Research Press, Champaign, Illinois, 1993.
3. E. Kübler-Ross, *On Death and Dying,* Macmillan Publishing Co., Inc., New York, 1969.
4. A. D. Wolfelt, Reconciliation Needs of the Mourner: Reworking a Critical Concept in Caring for the Bereaved, *Thanatos,* Spring 1988.

CHAPTER 3

AIDS Grief

What it is, why it's unique, what it means

In many ways AIDS grief is similar to grief that is related to any other terminal illness. AIDS grief differs because there are additional factors to consider that tend to complicate the grief. More often than not, the grief in AIDS survivors incorporates anger, fear, rage, and numbness to a greater extent than that seen in grief not associated with AIDS-related deaths. Even as we know that this grief may be complicated, an adequate definition for complicated grief has been elusive. The terminology is imprecise and inconsistent and it is often difficult to determine when mourning becomes complicated [1].

In many situations, mental health professionals use the term, "complicated grief" to describe certain behaviors and coping strategies that are perceived to be unhealthy. It is best to understand reactions to loss within the context of each mourner's experience without defining their grief as complicated. Labeling grief "complicated" does not necessarily imply that the grief is, or will be, pathological. There are many factors that contribute to complicated grief when dealing with deaths and losses related to AIDS, including the lengthy illness and the perception that the death was preventable.

When death occurs, the survivor experiences the loss of a significant relationship that may not have been recognized or validated by others. If this is the case, the subsequent grief is then "disenfranchised" and the mourner has a difficult time grieving openly [2]. Populations most greatly affected by

HIV/AIDS (gay, bisexual, substance addicted, imprisoned) may also be ones most disenfranchised and least accepted by society. In many of these communities, networks of chosen family units or supportive family-like structures, have formed. These units can consist of individuals and couples, adults and children, gay men, lesbians, and heterosexuals. Close-knit units provide support and caregiving to AIDS-affected individuals and survivors during the illness and during the mourning period after death occurs. The multiple losses related to AIDS that are experienced within these communities become even more devastating because of this closeness and isolation. What evolves is an unavoidable climate of loss to the community as a whole [3]. The irony is that the chosen family bonding that occurs becomes decimated by the pandemic.

Although much has been written about the emotional aspects of HIV/AIDS, not enough attention has been given to the feelings and experiences of the surviving partners, friends, or families of the deceased. Almost all survivors recognize that they could use support although they often feel so overwhelmed by the caregiving that they are unable to look for any resources. During the illness, some caregivers are aware of feelings of wanting to run away at each possible moment. Immediately they start feeling guilty for even having these thoughts. Others, during the dying process, want to be there every moment and caregiving becomes all consuming. They ignore all other aspects of their life. They sometimes wonder where the strength will come from to continue caregiving, supporting, and reassuring. Many people feel sad and alone. After a person dies of an AIDS-related illness, most survivors feel as if they have been through the most difficult time of their lives. As they looked back over many years of illness, they wonder how on earth they stayed involved as caregivers. They see that their life has changed in significant ways.

The grief of these survivors is rarely validated as many of their relationships are unaccepted, criticized, and gossiped about. The ability of most people to recognize and to respond to grief is further complicated by the lack of societal acceptance of a person bereaved by a death from AIDS-related illnesses. Western culture reacts with a great deal of discomfort to the feelings and topic of death and dying in the best of circumstances. Even when the relationship between the mourner and the deceased is clear and culturally sanctioned, there can be a guarded response from outsiders to the grief. Because of this discomfort, people often respond inadequately to a mourner's needs.

There are still relatively few places for mourners who are grieving deaths and losses from AIDS to go for consistent support and understanding. There is a pressing need for innovative approaches to providing psychosocial support for these survivors. Support is needed regardless of who the mourners are and what their medical situation entails. The issue of, and need for, available support has received some attention in the literature as the numbers of survivors increase. Support groups and psychosocial services have been established, mostly in urban areas heavily affected by HIV, but are rarely found elsewhere.

Some of the most effective and supportive groups are those established by and for people living with HIV/AIDS. One example of this type of group is "Being Alive", based in Los Angeles. Being Alive offers many support services to PLWA including advocacy programs and resources for daily needs. Organizations like these have provided a safe haven for many and can be started in cities where there are currently no services. Many established AIDS service organizations will offer help to those wanting to start a similar center in their home towns.

A problem exists because it is difficult at best for the unaffected to relate to these multiple losses. While a pandemic might be compared to a natural disaster in which many in a particular community are wiped out at one time, there are important differences when discussing the devastation of AIDS:

• When a disaster affects a community there is widespread emotional and financial support available. Individuals are rarely blamed and the whole community experiences a sudden, negative change. The change happens all at once and has a beginning, a middle, and an end. The disaster of AIDS is ongoing, and infected and affected individuals are in various stages of coping with its devastation. To date, it has no end. Those with AIDS are more likely to face discrimination, homophobia, and fear of contagion. They are also more likely to be seen as being individually responsible for their disease. They are then placed in a greater position of being stigmatized and socially isolated rather than supported.

• Mortality is linked to sexuality. People's conflicts and discomfort around sex, sexuality and AIDS make many less willing to offer support when death is AIDS related. Our society already disapproves of specific sexual behaviors. The belief that someone was infected with HIV during sexual relations, only increases the stigmatization and discrimination of those with a sexual orientation seen as unacceptable.

• It has become commonplace for those with AIDS to die in their twenties to forties. PLWA are often younger than forty-five. Young people are rarely equipped, psychologically or developmentally, to deal with death and multiple losses. The patient and his or her partners develop a sense of fatalism with a lack of enthusiasm for long-term goal planning. Results of one-time disasters more clearly define who is and who is not directly affected. This is not true of the AIDS disaster. Here there is a lack of sure knowledge of whether AIDS will continue to be part of the survivor's life. Factors are dependent upon his or her own HIV status and the status of those with whom there is close involvement.

• One-time disasters are finite with a pattern that includes the occurrence of the event, the rush to put things in order, the recovery period and the planning for the future free of that experience. In a community dealing with AIDS, because there is no cure and people are still dying, there is no post-trauma. AIDS grief is more profound because of this lack of an ending.

• Survivors tend to focus on the one loss perceived as the most significant in their lives. This loss might be a death or another kind of loss such as losing a job. They then treat this loss as the only one experienced. As a consequence, other losses may not be dealt with in a healthy fashion that could lead to resolution. Some people in a situation dealing with multiple losses are so overwhelmed that they often withdraw and are perceived as uncaring and unsympathetic. They appear to be unaffected by the death or deaths around them.

When Cary was asked how he was coping with all his friends' deaths, he told us, "I know they are all dead or dying, but I just forget about them and move on. There's nothing I can do about it anyway. What's the point of getting all upset?" His refusal to talk about his friends or to express his sad feelings increased his isolation. He became depressed and withdrew from most of his activities. He found himself unable to function at work. With support he was finally able to relate the changes in his behavior to the avoidance of the grief surrounding him. He began crying and sharing his intense feelings. He was able to talk about his friends; what they meant to him and how much he missed them. His performance at work improved and he became an advocate for learning how to grieve.

One unique aspect of AIDS grief is the tendency to focus on one loss. When a survivor focuses on a single loss, it is often because doing so allows him to "get a handle" on something he can manage to resolve. This could include grief feelings as well as trying to deal with an illness, e.g., Nate was told that his opportunistic infection, lymphoma, was no longer treatable. He appeared to have heard the doctor and just looked at him for a long time. Then he said, "Doc, will you take a look at this sore on my knee? What can you do about it?" The obvious sore seemed to Nate to be treatable whereas the idea of an untreatable disease was impossible to comprehend. He needed more time to absorb the news. Similarly, it is often overwhelming to deal with so many AIDS deaths and multiple losses. Grieving one death or loss in particular seems more manageable.

Other factors that contribute to the complicated grief and bereavement of AIDS include:

- Shortage of health care workers willing to treat PLWA, along with unavailable, and often inferior health care; health care that is usually available for people with other illnesses;
- Suicidal thoughts that are often common among PLWA;

- Fear of forming new relationships because so many friends are infected or at risk of infection; people are continually confronted with current and future deaths;
- Difficulty in differentiating between symptoms of grief and depression, and symptoms of HIV disease;
- Increasing dependency on over-utilized, under-funded community resources with constantly changing demographics;
- Homophobia, both internalized and externalized;
- Introduction of new medications that increase hope for survival for some but may be unsuccessful for others thereby creating additional anxiety and loss;
- Family conflicts created when men who died of AIDS have been bisexual, leading secret lives, and their wives or partners are unable to understand or accept this behavior.

The mental states of survivors of AIDS-related multiple losses are very complicated. It is important to realize that AIDS grief has been given many names that may not apply anymore. Survivors have been referred to at various times in this pandemic as "walking wounded," "worried well," suffering from "cumulative grief," or "post-traumatic stress disorder (PTSD)." "The replacement of pre-epidemic gay life by a death-saturated culture has caused a profound alteration of the social fabric and the reorganization of (gay) communal life" [4, p. 28].

In his book, *Reviving the Tribe*, Eric Rofes asks, "What keeps us from admitting that numbers of gay men might qualify for clinical diagnoses of PTSD? Many gay men throughout America are suffering a wide range of psychological responses that extend beyond bereavement and grief. Some may be experiencing simple grief, while many others are experiencing severe depression, mood disorders, constant trauma and PTSD." These sufferers should not be seen as abnormal. Rofes would like only to identify and treat their reactions with understanding and compassion.

AIDS grief has unique issues that have gone beyond gay men and now encompass people of all races, genders, ethnicities, and cultures. We must broaden our visions of how to define these issues and how to treat the survivors who are mourning.

REFERENCES

1. T. Rando, *Treatment of Complicated Mourning,* Research Press, Champaign, Illinois, 1993.
2. K. Doka, *Disenfranchised Grief: Recognizing Hidden Sorrow,* Lexington Books, Lexington, Massachusetts, 1989.
3. S. Schwartzberg, AIDS-Related Bereavement among Gay Men: The Inadequacy of Current Theories of Grief, *Psychotherapy, 29*:3, pp. 422-429, 1992.
4. E. Rofes, *Reviving the Tribe: Regenerating Gay Men's Sexuality and Culture in the Ongoing Epidemic,* Harrington Park Press: An Imprint of The Haworth Press, Inc., New York, 1996.

CHAPTER 4

AIDS Grief Groups

What they teach us

In 1982, I became a volunteer therapist at the AIDS Project Los Angeles. The Project had just begun offering support services to persons living with AIDS. This support included financial assistance, a food bank, advocacy through the complicated County social services, legal advice, and mental health support. These services were also offered on a more limited basis to the lovers, family members, and friends of these PLWA.

The PLWA were dying, and the people caring for them—the family and friends who survived—frequently found need for ongoing support, but none existed. Another volunteer therapist, Bill Fletcher, LCSW, and I recognized this need and, in 1983, began a series of grief recovery groups at the Project [1]. Our groups were among the first in the world to address the issue of grief related to AIDS deaths and losses. The support groups provided a place for survivors to share their experiences as they dealt with their loss or losses. They were able to express their needs and, hopefully, have them met. If all needs were not able to be taken care of, at least many found comfort being with others in similar circumstances. Since that time I have been doing supportive psychotherapy with this survivor population on an individual basis as well as in support groups. I am called upon frequently to train volunteers at AIDS service organizations, present in-service training programs to their staffs and, to facilitate support groups for these agency counselors.

For many years the group members were mainly gay men who were the surviving partners or friends of someone who had died of AIDS-related illnesses. The men were mostly Caucasian, well-educated and ranging in age from twenty-two years to sixty-four years. As the deaths increased, others mourning those who died of AIDS-related illnesses began attending the support groups. Participants now included business partners, co-workers and employers, friends, family members, and those who had been "buddies." (Buddies were volunteers from the AIDS organizations who helped give care to the PLWA.) Our group seemed to be the only place for these mourners to come for support and understanding.

We questioned the advisability of starting a support group with a mixed population as opposed to a group for gay men and one for mourners who were not gay. We finally decided to mix the participants because we were the only group in the city at the time that was dealing with grief from AIDS. Some attendees were skeptical at first although they did continue to attend. As long as we, as co-therapists, were comfortable with the decision to accept all AIDS mourners, most of the people were also comfortable. Many of the groups worked well, although we did have moments when we questioned our judgment.

One mourner in a mixed group was a mother whose son had died of AIDS-related illness. She came to the group in deep grief and with great anger. This anger was frequently directed at the gay men in the group. For two sessions they just listened to her and didn't even discuss their grief. By the third session, Henry couldn't take it anymore. He exploded at her yelling, "My grief is as great for my lover as yours is for your son. We all have a lot of grief and we are all angry too. So, it's about time you listened to us!" The two of them went at each other yelling and crying. Everyone else was stunned by this outburst. As the session neared its end the two of them stared at each other in stony silence.

We thought we'd never see either of them again but they both came to the next session. She started talking about how she never understood her son and wished he wasn't gay so he'd still be alive. Henry started talking about how his mother never understood him either. At times during the next several sessions they began dialoging with each other, hugging each other, and having coffee after the group meetings. They subsequently supported each other as adoptive mother and son for a long period. Having a safe environment to explore their relationship with their son and lover as well as with each other, allowed them to come to a mutual understanding that was supportive to both. The other group members were also able to work out issues with their own parents by observing and sharing in the conversations. This particular mixed group was quite successful. We decided that the most important element to a successful group was the level of comfort we as therapists have with our decisions. We create an environment of safety and acceptance, and then participants will feel welcome.

Caregivers from all walks of life attended the groups but the gay male population was the population most greatly affected by AIDS in the United States in the early 1980s. We could see that the grief issues for these men were quite different from those for the general grieving population. Not only were individuals struggling with an incurable, terminal disease, they were living in a community that was, and still is, affected by huge losses. It became clear that "Gay Grief" needed to be defined and supported.

Gay men often lack acceptance in their home communities so they leave home estranged from their families. Cities with large gay populations accept and welcome them, and they will settle in these places. When they become terminally ill and need care, however, some tend to call upon their biological families for assistance. When the family members arrive, they often find themselves dealing with a grown child telling them simultaneously that he is gay and dying. The families are often overwhelmed. Taking care of dying sons, trying to comprehend what is happening, sorting out their son's relationships and property, while simultaneously making funeral arrangements is overwhelming. There is no time to deal with the emotional complexity of the situation.

Parents of the deceased men were referred to us and would call to express an interest in attending the group. They appreciated knowing that support was available when they wanted to reach out. Because they frequently lived out of town they rarely came to any of the group meetings.

Since death from AIDS was, and still is, taboo, the parents often kept secret the cause of their son's death when they returned to their hometowns. They usually lied about the diagnosis so they could receive the support from friends and other family members that might not be available if people knew the real reason for the death. They also were trying to protect themselves and other family members from the stigma and social ostracism that may be present just because they are associated with someone who had died of an AIDS-related illness. One doesn't have to have a gay son who died this way to deal with this issue. After the funeral, these mourners had to live with the guilt and anger and the fear of being discovered in their lies. Some of the mothers called us looking for support when the secret became too painful to keep. They needed someone to talk to about their child and we were available. They knew we understood.

Mrs. Miller tearfully called us daily. Guilt consumed her and she felt responsible for her son's death from AIDS. She said, "I really tried hard to be understanding about Jim's gay life. I hoped my understanding would help him. But now I know it killed him." Remorse overcame her after his death. She was convinced that he would still be alive if she had only stopped him in some way from being gay. Sharing this fear with us and hearing our responses helped her slowly accept that it was never in her power to "stop him from being gay."

As the years went by and the number of deaths from AIDS increased, the make-up of the groups changed even more. Groups were formed just for women, or for those who were dealing with many deaths. Mental health counselors established groups wherever and whenever the need arose. Survivors included not only life partners, co-workers, employers, and friends of the deceased gay men, but also, husbands of women who died of AIDS-related illnesses, and members of different ethnic communities. Many of the mourners were themselves infected with HIV and were becoming ill. As facilitators, we chose to have the group off-limits to any person abusing drugs or alcohol. Their behavior in group was often too disruptive. These people were referred to agencies better equipped to deal with their multiple problems.

In the mid-eighties we became aware of the euphemisms in the obituary column of the *Los Angeles Times* describing deaths from AIDS. For example, "John Doe died of cancer," or of lymphoma, pneumonia, or meningitis. The obituary often goes on to say that the deceased person, often under age forty, is survived by a *life partner* of "x" years more or less. All these descriptions seem to indicate that the deceased died of one of the opportunistic illnesses related to AIDS. Since we often knew the deceased and the cause of death, we realized that the survivors did not want the sexual orientation and HIV status of the deceased to be known. AIDS deaths stigmatized the families. The rights and needs of the survivors seem to conflict with those of the deceased. The gay dead person was often buried "straight."

The number of deaths increased as the years passed and, the cause of death reported in the obituaries became somewhat more accurate. We began seeing "Death from complications of AIDS." AIDS is the name of a syndrome that takes away the power of the body to fight off opportunistic infections that cause death. How simplistic! What could be more complicated than these opportunistic infections? Not only were the obituaries becoming more accurate, they were also seen more and more frequently. It is obvious that the need for grief work will continue for a long time.

Deaths from AIDS were now increasing worldwide. Pandemic, not epidemic, became the chosen word for this devastating disease. Conferences were held all over the world and the attendees of these international meetings were hungry for knowledge about the multiple losses of AIDS. They, too, realized that AIDS grief was in need of special recognition. We began presenting our findings and ideas starting with a comparison of the types of grief groups offered by us and those offered by the traditional, non AIDS-related, grieving community. The findings helped to further verify the need for understanding of the unique issues of AIDS grief .

Comparison of Grief Support Groups: Non-AIDS-Related Versus AIDS-Related

Non-AIDS Grief Groups	AIDS Grief Groups
Majority of participants are women age 50 or older.	Majority are men frequently younger than 45.
Members encompass a cross-section of society. They are sometimes shunned by non-grievers because they are reminders of death.	Members come from a sub-culture with a lifestyle already condemned by society. Also likely to be shunned as possible HIV carriers.
Low self-esteem and guilt are common.	Low self-esteem and guilt are often made worse by internalizing society's homophobic attitudes.
Members are likely to have a network of family, friends, and children to lend support during the mourning period.	Deceased is often the survivors only real "family." Biological family may be non-existent or distant emotionally and geographically. Even if they are sympathetic, their sexual orientation is usually different than that of the survivors. May not understand the affectional bond that has been cut. Family and friends may resent and refuse to accept the survivor, causing greater sense of abandonment and isolation.
Survivors may have feelings of guilt about having caused their partner's final illness or death but it is rarely related to direct transmission of a fatal infection.	Survivors often suffer from guilt over behaviors that may have contributed to the deceased's infection with HIV and subsequent death.
When a spouse dies, many older widows and widowers are confronted with the reality of their own deaths sometime in the future. Issues such as "Who will be there for me?" increase in importance.	For the AIDS bereaved the future is more uncertain. Those who lack family support and doubt the possibility of another long-term relationship, see a lonely death as the likely reality. Ongoing death is common throughout their community and a person often feels as if he is the only one left.

Non-AIDS Grief Groups	AIDS Grief Groups
The role of widow or widower is well-defined in society. They have an identity and a title, and their bereavement is a clearly understood time of distress.	No societal approval exists for gay marital relationships and no tradition is yet available for gay mourning. No descriptive title identifies the mourner who may not be able to express feelings as people may question the intense feelings for someone who was "just a friend."
Traditional male/female roles usually have been assigned in the relationship and the survivor must assume unfamiliar role obligations.	Less role-playing occurs in gay relationships. Gay men are accustomed to living independently, managing diverse roles. If death exposes homosexuality, the survivor must deal with the additional loss of the "straight" role.
The institution of marriage has certain guarantees for survivors' financial security such as inheritance laws, Social Security, and other benefits to next of kin.	Financial benefits are not guaranteed to survivors. Formal legal arrangements are necessary for jointly acquired property that will be left to the survivor.
Anticipatory grief may be eased during periods of hospitalization as spouses are welcome at the bedside. Displays of affection are accepted and supported by the hospital staff.	Partners are often barred from Intensive Care units and are made to feel unwelcome in the hospital. Displays of affection arouse hostility among staff and other patients.
It is assumed that survivors will be in charge of funeral services and burial arrangements.	Surviving partners are often excluded from funeral plans and deceased is sometimes buried "straight" with no acknowledgment of ties to gay life.
Discussions of sexuality are infrequent.	Discussions of sexuality are frequent and center on sexual frustrations and fears of resuming sex due to possible infection with HIV.

Non-AIDS Grief Groups	AIDS Grief Groups
Sexual attraction to another group member sometimes occurs but is not likely as most members are female. They are not looking for a partner from within the group.	Opportunities for sexual attraction are present because of the same-sex orientation in the group. Members may form premature bonds or exceed group boundaries with others.
Re-entry to life and re-socialization are difficult but acceptable goals after a suitable period of time. It is aceptable for widows and widowers to join in social activities after a suitable period of time.	Re-entry and re-socialization are also difficult and in addition are compli-cated by HIV/AIDS. One is more likely to be confronted with illness and death in great numbers.
Many community resources provide support during grief: clergy, physi-cians, private agencies, and therapists. Usually someone who has had grief-work experience can be found.	Community resources exist for the current population of PLWA; however, those that do often have limited experi-ence with, or understanding of, grief work. If this population participates in grief groups not sensitive to their needs, their discomfort increases and they feel unwelcome.
Religious organizations acknowledge the bereaved's relationship to the deceased and provide comfort and the opportunity to say good-bye in a formalized way.	Gay people are often ostracized from formal religious organizations and have to plan their own memorials and services.

This comparison supports the assumption that the non-AIDS related group of mourners can rely more on built-in societal support systems. The limits of these systems in the male homosexual community give rise to many unique issues and create a need for specialized interventions. For gay grief issues to mirror non-gay grief issues, increased education, recognition of homophobic attitudes, changes in societal acceptance, and anti-discriminatory behavior need to occur. Until that time, this group is maintaining its isolation and developing its own traditions and rituals related to death, dying, and grief.

Many topics exist that are possible to discuss in bereavement support groups. Besides defining what grief and bereavement means, the participants can discuss their relationships with professional caregivers and the community they encountered during the illness of the deceased and after the death. Sharing these experiences helps remind people of the meaning and value of their relationship with the deceased and often diffuses the anger remaining from previous unpleasant circumstances. They can explore and understand family interactions. Multiple losses in the community and the reactions to the way people are surviving can be shared and rituals can be developed. As one goes on with life, the implications for mortality and spirituality are put into perspective by this sharing. Talking about distressing experiences and learning to let go, exploring future relationships and how to find social support are also valuable topics.

It is important not only to talk about the deceased, but also to define the role the dead person plays in the life of the survivors. Tony Walter suggests that it would seem that the dead live on without impairing the functioning of the living [2]. Grievers who understand and accept that this is within the normal process of grief, can then integrate their loved ones into their lives without feeling as if they are being foolish or crazy. Walter suggests the following ways for this involvement to happen. The deceased can be in the life of the survivor:

- As a role model,
- To give guidance in specific situations,
- To help clarify the values of the survivor, and
- As a valued part of the survivor's biography.

Finally, discussions in the support groups of what death taught can affirm the value of life. Perhaps, lessons learned will even predict what a mourner needs in order to move on.

> Loss came around with the seasons, blew into the house when you opened the windows, piled up in the bottom desk and dresser drawers, accumulated in the back of closets, heaped in the basement starting by the

furnace, and came creeping up the basement stairs. Loss grew as you did without your consent; your losses mounted beside you like earthworm castings. No willpower could prevent someone dying. And no willpower could restore someone dead, breathe life into that frame and set it going again in the room with you to meet your eyes. That was the fact of death [3, p. 288].

REFERENCES

1. S. Klein and W. Fletcher, Gay Grief: An Examination of Its Uniqueness Brought to Light by the AIDS Crisis, *Journal of Psychosocial Oncology, 4*:3, pp. 15-25, 1987.
2. T. Walter, A New Model of Grief: Bereavement and Biography, *Mortality, 1*:1, 1996.
3. A. Dillard, *An American Childhood*, HaperCollins, New York, 1987.

CHAPTER 5

Multiple Losses of AIDS:
Not Just Deaths

The presence of absence is everywhere.

(from an obituary)

We had been sitting in comfortable silence for some moments. She reached slowly over and her touch was light, incredibly smooth, and unexpectedly comforting. She laid her hand on top of mine. "You know," she said quietly, "every one of my friends is dead now." Without looking up at her I said "So are mine Grandma."

Kermit Berg, a graphic artist,
personal correspondence, 1991

Multiple loss, in the context of HIV/AIDS as I use the term, is defined as losing many people to AIDS-related death. When I write of multiple losses, I am referring to all losses a survivor can relate to along with death [1]. Gay men, who are survivors of AIDS-related multiple loss, talk of going through their address books systematically crossing out the names of those who have died. This experience has been referred to at various times as a "defining moment" in the process of realizing the magnitude of the human loss implicit in the AIDS pandemic. Examples of multiple deaths and the many other losses in the gay community are forerunners of what other communities will face as AIDS continues its course. Many of the experiences in the gay community are representative of all multiple loss issues surrounding people who are stigmatized and discriminated against because they have HIV/AIDS.

Kenny, who died of an AIDS-related opportunistic infection in 1994, told me, "Since 1981, I've lost, at last count, slightly more than 150 friends and acquaintances; two lovers, one employer, and seven co-workers."

Tom tested HIV-positive in 1985. He shared that his "first close friend died in 1986. Total number of friends lost is something I don't wish to contemplate. Four or five close friends a year, numerous acquaintances, and co-workers also dead."

Leon McKusick, a psychologist in San Francisco who died of AIDS-related illness, wrote about two paradoxes caused by multiple losses. "The first paradox of HIV loss is that the need for social support can be clouded by the deterioration of social support networks themselves. Current losses are reducing the number of peers from whom to draw support." The second paradox he describes is that there is no cure but there are promising treatments. Many infected men become more depressed as the losses increase and this depression and hopelessness may interfere with seeking treatment and treatment compliance, thereby leading to more deaths. As time goes on, the deaths still continue, but there seems to be an adaptive process occurring. The responses seen in survivors are more like what is seen in post-traumatic stress where people tend to feel numb and detached and have limited interest in pursuing goals or new relationships.

Death is now a regular, normal event in the gay community. Ironically, for some men, the amount of depression seems to lessen with each death. However, the grief continues and so does the distress. Distress along with the grief, is especially felt by those who are HIV-positive or are caregivers of PLWA. They live with chronic stress and tend to access support systems available through AIDS service organizations to help them acquire skills to survive. Perhaps social support interventions will reduce psychological distress in these affected and infected individuals. Karl Goodkin, M.D., suggests that there may be other equally plausible possibilities for the lower frequency of complicated bereavement reactions observed over time [3]. For example, a greater acceptance of death in the age of HIV/AIDS has developed. Maybe there is a change in the way people react rather than a true reduction in bereavement responses.

The increasing number of survivors dealing with the ever increasing deaths from AIDS need a clear definition of the meaning of multiple loss; a constellation of physical, emotional, and psychosocial issues swirling around waiting to be defined and understood. The responses to multiple losses are common to survivors regardless of whether or not they have resolved or unresolved grief. It is a different phenomenon than a grief reaction. To better understand how it is different, I am defining multiple losses in a way that includes and reflects the losses other than death experienced by all who are members of any decimated population. With a diagnosis of AIDS, the following types of loss interact and impact one another:

- Loss of validation from society, often including the loss of family support due to rejection and fear,
- Loss of health,
- Loss of physical and emotional well-being,
- Loss of sense of community,
- Loss of sexual freedom,
- Loss of employment stability due to the stigma attached to HIV/AIDS,
- Loss of (discretionary) income due to illness-related expenses,
- Loss of free time due to constraints of caregiving,
- Loss of privacy and personal power resulting from the outing of sexual orientation when HIV status becomes known,
- Loss of caregiver role when the PLWA dies,
- Loss of persons still alive due to personality changes caused by the infection and the disease,
- Loss of one's history,
- Loss of a sense of world order,
- Loss of role models and leaders who became activists in the cause,
- Loss of dreams of growing old together, and,
- Loss of hope for the future.

As these frequent and multiple losses are experienced, survivors may find themselves withdrawing and turning inward, away from possible support systems. The deep and intense emotions felt can be devastating. The grieving persons might begin feeling some or all of the following long-term and possibly irreparable consequences:

- They may experience emotional numbing, depression, and an inability to express feelings. Feelings of pessimism, cynicism, fatalism, and insecurity are common. As these may be new feelings and behaviors, survivors believe that something is seriously wrong with them and they will never get better.

  "Every death is a reminder of my own mortality." Before Mac died in 1995 he shared with me that he felt "shell-shocked, angry, scared, numb, like I'm looking in a mirror. I isolate in defense. I dream of escaping it all, moving to a cabin in the mountains where the nightmare would slowly fade. 'Who's next?' is the most frequent question that crosses my mind. 'Where am I in line?' runs closely behind."

- Multiple loss differs from normal bereavement in several important ways. People who have faced loss after loss in a relatively short period of time, cannot realistically be expected to bounce back as quickly as those experiencing fewer losses over longer periods of time. There is a decreased likelihood that the grief of each loss can be resolved before the next loss occurs. Each experience of grief is compounded by all the losses that have come before the last one. There is the further complication of the anticipation of more deaths to come. It is difficult to find enough time between these traumas to work through the complex grief process.

- Death from AIDS is rarely sudden. The prolonged progression of the disease offers opportunities for *anticipatory grief*: a type of grief that occurs before the actual death. Anticipatory grief can influence the intensity of the feelings associated with death. As a patient begins the living/dying process, the loved one frequently begins to feel this type of grief. The person they knew is changing and disappearing. They begin grieving that loss. They may begin to wish for a peaceful death and relief from suffering. The length of time before death may also allow them a greater chance to begin to let go of the dying person. If there is time to say good-bye and each person is able to talk about his or her feelings, the grieving period after death is sometimes more manageable. If the significant other is also HIV infected, the current loss will be mourned as well as losses to come. This includes their own illness and death. The grief will be more difficult and painful if there is unfinished business, resentment, unexpressed anger, or a troubled relationship with the deceased.

- Those caregivers and friends who repeatedly watch friends die after prolonged illnesses, may find themselves developing indifference or what I call "compassionate detachment." This detachment often is connected to feelings of numbness and an attitude of "I just don't care anymore." I believe that detaching like this is what allows people to continue involvement with those who need them. The prolonged emotional numbing commonly described by those experiencing multiple losses is a natural result of surviving ongoing devastation. It is not a lack of sensitivity or caring. A friend of a colleague of mine seasons his indifference with morbid humor. He said, "Honey, I'm burying so many of my friends that I've decided to put the morgue on speed dial on my phone."

- Continuing deaths of friends and acquaintances has a cumulative effect on survivors. It has been documented that surviving multiple loss puts one at greater risk for depression [2]. Many survivors experience changes in sleeping or eating patterns, in activity or energy level, and in involvement with work, friends, and family. Experiencing these symptoms is reason to seek counseling and supportive therapy. The comments of some survivors of multiple losses reflect the relationship between so many deaths and feelings of depression:

> Often I will think of someone who would be good to talk to and then I'll realize they are dead. I used to just get sad and depressed about this and try to avoid the feelings. Now I try to remember the person and think about what they might say. If I'm sad and depressed, well then, I am. Others will just have to deal with it (Tom West, personal communication, 1993).

Ian received a phone call from a friend asking him to attend a memorial service the following Saturday. Ian asked, "What time?" His friend responded, "Aren't you even going to ask who died?"

> I began to feel the "snowball" effect when these deaths begin to happen back to back. I began to feel overwhelmed and disloyal in the sense that I haven't done enough to pay tribute to each friend. The large number of deaths forces you to use more impersonal coping techniques, like lists or one memorial service every six months to cover all. You begin to develop a Teflon coating. It forces you to prioritize your friends and loved ones (Lonnie Cunningham, personal communication, 1992).

> Sadly, it seems to get easier. After my 40th memorial service, I decided to stop going. By this time, of course, they'd become slightly less festive than tea dances. No somber colors. Everyone will be cheerful. Balloons are a must, darling. Music. Dancing. "God's picking all his flowers at once" it was said "but by God at least we're assured there will be someone up there to have a fully stocked bar by the time we get there!" Mac said it best, "We've gone from a let-us-set-aside-this-day-to-remember-Fred frame of mind to Memorial? Yeah, I can probably make it if it's near a market and a dry cleaners . . . I've GOT to pick up some cat food." I still pray for each departed soul, but it's no longer a kneel-by-the-bed and weep situation, but rather, Well, Lord, here comes another one. Show him around, would ya? (Ken Poe, personal communication, 1992).

The support groups we facilitated started as bereavement groups but soon became more. Some of the participants began experiencing other losses including their own loss of health as they found out that they were HIV-positive and began developing opportunistic infections that led to AIDS. The group members began exploring how their lives were affected by these additional losses.

Feelings and thoughts that emerged define *Multiple Loss Characteristics.*

ANGER AND RAGE

As one man struggling with these issues described it: "Despair is a word that comes frequently to mind. These combined losses leave a sense that all foundations' one had are now removed" (Reece, personal communication, 1992). Not surprisingly, anger often becomes a predominant emotion in AIDS grief. People are angry because of many of the following:

- the youthfulness of those being cut down in the prime of life, the difficulty of dealing with loss after loss,
- the abandonment by those considered to be part of a support system,
- the discrimination frequently found in the workplace, and
- the stress associated with the frequent denial of insurance and medical benefits.

Anger also originates in an awareness of the ravages of the disease—contagion, neurological complications, protracted illness, and disfigurement.

RESENTMENT

It is not uncommon for many survivors to experience intense resentment about the seemingly endless memorial services to attend. If the choice is made to skip one or more of these services, the guilt feelings are difficult to deal with. Making the choice to not go creates confusion because attending such services is an appropriate way to pay respects and say good-bye. Survivors of multiple loss who attend services find their emotions stirred up causing the re-experiencing of previous intense feelings of grief. Remembering the pain and sadness tends to make people avoid any experience where that may happen again. The benefit of seeing this as a cathartic situation in the grief process is often overlooked.

Some group members even complained about the monotony and predictability of memorial services, and commented on the "deadness" (emotional numbing) they felt. Allen Barnett captures the despair of gay men who have buried too many friends and lovers in "The 'Times' As It Knows Us": "But the words we use now reek of old air in churches. . . . Our condolences are arid as leaves. We are actors who have over-rehearsed our lines" [4]. Facing multiple deaths makes it increasingly difficult to offer condolences. The usual words sound repetitious and trite and make one feel insincere. People wonder how many ways there are to say "I'm sorry."

VICTIMIZATION AND PUNISHMENT

While PLWA object to being called victims, they acknowledge feeling victimized and punished by society. Babies with AIDS are called "innocent victims" while our culture tells gay men that they brought it upon themselves. People forget that there were a large number of infected persons before anyone knew what this disease was capable of doing.

Why me? Why us? Why all my friends? Why those I love? Life punishes those with different sexual orientations and perceived unacceptable behaviors. There also seems to be a belief that gay men are supposed be more compliant, motivated, and well educated about AIDS since the disease has affected them so greatly. The fact that they continue to become infected increases homophobic reactions. The result of this blaming is that those feeling victimized want to lash out at those perceived to be attacking them. This can lead to socially irresponsible behaviors, impulsive decision making, and increased isolation. It is a time to discourage people from making precipitous moves like selling homes and quitting jobs without thinking through the consequences. Unfortunately, at times like these, they are most incapable of seeking guidance and listening to advice.

PANIC, SELF-DOUBT, AND LOSS OF CONTROL

One consequence of the AIDS pandemic is that individuals belonging to populations engaging in risky behavior, have difficulty believing that they have control over their life. While many affected men have become more sensitive to death in general, they are also left with substantial feelings of insecurity and vulnerability. One man complained of "feeling like rubber," commenting that he was "being pulled in too many directions at once." He felt totally unable to "firm up" his life and maintain a "sense of positive meaning and productivity." He felt a loss of control and of being totally overwhelmed by the number of friends who continued to die. He forced himself to visit the sick to reduce the guilt he experienced when he neglected his friends (Lonnie Cunningham, personal communication 1991).

SOCIAL ISOLATION

When one experiences repeated grief, there is an ongoing fear that any investment in new relationships will only lead to subsequent grief and emotional pain. People often resist developing new sources of badly needed social support. This sense of isolation is further intensified as one withdraws and support systems deteriorate. The survivor now faces his pain and grief in even more isolation than need be.

Survivors may be conflicted as they become aware of feelings of isolation and abandonment while simultaneously withdrawing from social support networks. Without awareness of this confusing contradiction, the deterioration of the survivors social support networks may be so extensive that, for some survivors of multiple loss, there will be limited support for dealing with grief issues.

The concern of health professionals is that these survivors are at great risk for increased illness. At least one study has documented the fact that suppression of the immune system accompanies bereavement and social support has a direct effect on improving one's health status and behavior [5]. Awareness of this phenomenon can help those in contact with the grieving survivor direct and encourage his or her participation in supportive activities.

Fears of "setting oneself up" for future losses need to be examined. These fears may also prevent the survivor from taking advantage of support that is available. Taking the risk of talking to others and finding support groups allows the survivors to celebrate their capacity for caring deeply about others. As survivors get the support they need, they will feel more hopeful and will have more energy for giving back to the world. Survivors feel permission to celebrate life once again.

POSSIBLE CHARACTERISTICS OF
MULTIPLE LOSS

- Feelings of numbness, anger, isolation, abandonment, guilt, disbelief, depression, and rage.

- Resentment over never-ending memorial services, constant hospital visits, and reminders of sickness and death.

- Feeling victimized and punished.

- Panic, self-doubt, and loss of control. Feeling loss of interest in former activities.

- Social isolation. Withdrawal from social support systems.

- Fear of losing the ability to feel anything or express one's feelings when each successive person dies.

- Possibly behaving in socially irresponsible ways with self-destructive overtones.

- Preoccupation with one's own mortality. Increased anxiety and other feelings associated with personal death awareness.

- Survivors' deep sadness that he or she will be the only one left alive in the community.

REFERENCES

1. S. J. Klein, AIDS-Related Multiple Loss Syndrome, *Illness, Crises and Loss,* Vol. 4, The Charles Press Publishers, Philadelphia, Pennsylvania, pp. 13-25, 1994.
2. L. McKusick and R. Hilliard, Multiple Loss Accounts for Worsening Distress in a Community Hard Hit by AIDS, *Plenary Paper presented at the 1991 International Conference on AIDS,* Florence, Italy, p. 4, 1991.
3. K. Goodkin et al., Bereavement and HIV Infection, *International Review of Psychiatry, 8,* pp. 201-216, 1996.
4. A. Barnett, The 'Times' As It Knows Us, in *Short Stories From the AIDS Crisis,* S. O. Warner (ed.), Citadel Press, 1996.
5. S. Schleifer, S. Keller, M. Cameron, J. Thornton, and M. Stein, Suppression of Lymphocyte Stimulation Following Bereavement, *Journal of the American Medical Association, 250*:3, July 15, 1988.

CHAPTER 6

Problem Solving in the Gay Community

Lessons for other HIV/AIDS communities

The pandemic is now well into its second decade. The large number of survivors of AIDS-related deaths has shown that standard beliefs about grief and mourning need to be questioned. Old truths no longer apply. Survivors experience both traditional grief reactions and new patterns of grief that appear to be unique in deaths related to AIDS. Bereavement is especially prevalent among gay men due to the disproportionate numbers who have died of AIDS-related illnesses. The effect of this grief appears to be cumulative causing increased physical and psychological distress. The gay community has found solutions for some of the problems even though many problems have, as yet, no solutions.

Gay mourners, particularly, have special needs and it is important to understand gay grief. Gay men today grieve not only for their dead and dying friends but also for a way of life that is gone and may never come again. The men are searching for and finding new ways to relate that may pose fewer health risks. The ability to express freely and casually, a powerful human need, sex, is no longer possible without the fear of fatal consequences. The satisfaction that intimate contact can bring is changed for gay men as well as for any sexual active person.

The grieving experience for gay survivors of individuals who have died from AIDS has added components that are different from the traditional models of grief and mourning as described earlier in this book. There are numerous obstacles to overcome in order to resolve grief. These obstacles apply to other infected/ affected populations, but the gay community is used here as an example of one that has come up with effective problem solving.

A gay survivor may find himself socially stigmatized. Individuals outside the gay community may stereotype him as gay (with negative connotations), as an IV drug user, or as a sexually promiscuous person. Many unknowing observers automatically assume that a gay survivor is HIV-positive. A colleague of mine recently suffered a disabling illness. Because of his altered physical appearance, people constantly approach him telling him how sorry they are. They say, "I didn't realize you have AIDS." He has come out as an HIV-negative person to encourage discussion of the prejudices and judgments people make without real knowledge of someone's situation. He has seen first hand that gay men are treated disdainfully. People accuse them of reckless behavior saying, "You should have known better." "You are spreading this horrible disease." These social dynamics and this mistreatment may prevent the gay survivor from attending community grief support groups that are not specifically gay or AIDS-related. Feeling unfairly judged makes it more difficult for survivors to seek help.

Those gay men who do receive support become more comfortable asserting their rights in relationships. They have established protocols to help insure that the wishes of the deceased will be carried out. In the early years of the epidemic, after the death of a partner, the survivor was often ignored when jointly owned property was assumed to belong only to the deceased. The family frequently removed this property against the stated wishes of both parties. The frequent losses of jointly owned property caused gay men to seek legal advice to prevent this from continuing. Many lawyers and legal clinics have offered pro bono services to set up wills, trusts, and other legal documents to protect partners. Families have contested these documents but have not been successful in reversing the intentions of the deceased when the papers were properly written. AIDS service organizations have offered their clients legal services so that there is a lessening of problems, though these services are often only available in communities knowledgeable about these issues. Legal protection offers much needed peace of mind during the time of bereavement..

Elliott and his partner, Tim, had made detailed, but not legalized, funeral plans. When Tim's family arrived, they completely ignored the arrangements. They took Tim's body back to their hometown for burial. Elliott's sense of guilt at having let his lover down was overwhelming. "I felt so helpless. They just swooped in and took over. Tim's family loved me. They included us in all the family celebrations and we traveled all over with them. They told me that they loved me like their son. Who could have possibly imagined that they would do this to us. What am I going to do now? Tim is not where he wanted to be and I can't visit him or put flowers on his grave." Listening to Elliott's sad story impressed on the other group members the importance of having up-to-date legal documents that made their wishes clear.

Many of the men planned their own funeral services down to the last detail and made these plans legal to avoid any confusion after they died. When legal documents specify funeral arrangements, the deceased's wishes can be carried out. Otherwise, the family often appears and takes the remains without friend's knowledge or approval. Seeing the person dead is part of the first task of acceptance and not having the body available to pay last respects causes additional stress for the survivors. Mourners are encouraged to have memorial services even if the family has made funeral plans that do not include some of the survivors. These "Celebrations of Life" of the deceased offer closure to those who attend. Accomplishing closure allows the task of grieving to resolution to continue.

For a period of time, many hospitals had separate wards for AIDS patients, most of who were gay men. Doctors specializing in this disease are often gay and the nursing staff frequently volunteers to be on this service. The issue of friends and lovers being allowed in the hospital rooms in an intimate way, showing affection, became a moot point. However, since the development and use of new medications, discovered in 1995, PLWA are experiencing less frequent hospitalizations and separate AIDS units in hospitals are not needed in the same numbers. Many AIDS units and hospices have, in fact, closed.

The combination of protease inhibitors and the previously approved AIDS drugs reduce the patient's viral load so that it may be undetectable in some PLWA. This is important to know because viral load testing is turning out to be a better predictor of the future course of HIV infection than the previously thought T-cell counts. A new lease on life is now given to patients with lower viral loads. They are noticing improvement in their health and well-being. The disease is being kept under control for some and is being managed as a chronic illness. PLWA on these medical regimens are now seeing their physicians mainly for compliance in taking the complicated dosages (Mark Katz, M.D., personal communication, 1997). It is not as easy as it sounds. There are not yet answers to many questions: (e.g., When is the best time to take protease inhibitors? What is the best way? Which one? What combinations? Will resistance develop? Then what?)

And the cost of the new drugs is very high, being prohibitive for many of those living with AIDS. The low or no income patients who are being cared for by county services or those who have no insurance cannot afford these drugs. They often do not seek care until they are gravely ill. When patients do need hospitalization, they find that the hospital staff's level of tolerance for affection is related to the level of acceptance of gay's in the community. The irony is that when an AIDS patient does need to be hospitalized, he or she is most likely, once again, to be placed in a general medical service room with a non-AIDS patient. This is a step backward. If these patients and their visitors feel rejection and discrimination the care received and the mourning period when the patient dies will be negatively affected. There is a sense of injustice and a carryover of anger and rage.

With this possible new longevity for some PLWA comes a new problem recently coined "survivor panic" or "future shock" by those whose lives have changed, drastically and suddenly. There are many psychological issues and re-entry problems. In a recent article in the *Los Angeles Times*, an AIDS patient is quoted as saying, "I realized this week that I have been prepared to die, but I'm not prepared to live. I know it may sound crazy." In this same article, the author, Clifford Rothman writes, "But it doesn't sound crazy. Not to the thousands who have put affairs in order, written wills, bought cemetery plots, said their good-byes, sold life insurance policies, maxed out credit cards, given up jobs, gone on disability—only to find themselves getting better, thanks to these new drugs" [1].

Their hopes are raised cautiously, but raised nevertheless, because they remember other promising treatments that failed. As with any new treatments, some patients will respond and others will not. People who are getting better do not know what to do with their lives and they feel as if they are starting over. They have to think about getting a job, earning a living, and saving for a still uncertain future. Those who are not responding to the drugs blame themselves, for some reason believing that it is their fault that the medications have failed. They feel happy and envious at the same time for their friends who are responding to the drugs while their own hopelessness and frustration continue. The normal anger of grief turns to rage and depression in those for whom the medication came too late. Mental health management is now a goal for these PLWA as they continue to ride the roller coaster of HIV/AIDS. AIDS service organizations are planning support around wellness not illness.

These new medications bring a cure for hopelessness but not yet a cure for this disease. Being vigilant and taking personal responsibility for one's behavior is still the most important treatment. Safe sexual practices must continue in order to prevent infection. When people see AIDS or any other disease, as treatable and no longer a certain death, they tend to be less vigilant in their behavior.

Even with these life-affirming medications, there is still a large grieving population in the gay community. This turn of events is bound to affect bereavement services as the efforts of the counselors will be going toward the PLWA. Now, support services for bereaved gay men explore the possibility of new relationships within the context of this hopeful environment. There may be less chance that a new partner will become sick and die but those survivors who are HIV-positive still worry about infecting someone else and being a burden if they were to become ill. Until they can resolve their grief, it would be best to avoid becoming serious about another partner. A repeat of the pain of loss would be overwhelming.

Those who test HIV-negative have important issues that have to be recognized and supported. They worry about being a constant caregiver, about becoming infected, or about whether to have a relationship with anyone who may be HIV-positive. All of these factors and more, contributed to much uncertainty in the community.

Years of lobbying and activism in the gay community have resulted in AIDS-in-the-workplace education and anti-discrimination laws. These laws have begun to take effect in many cities resulting in increased familiarity with AIDS-related issues for gays and nongays alike. As members of society overcome their fear and ignorance of AIDS issues, they are more likely to recognize and validate gay grief, and to integrate survivors into the community at large.

REFERENCE

1. C. Rothman, A World Turned Upside-Down: With Promising New Drugs, are HIV Patients Ready for Life? *Los Angeles Times,* Section E, Tuesday, November 5, 1996.

CHAPTER 7

Survivors: HIV-Negative, HIV-Positive, Status Unknown

Why it makes a difference

Walt Odets, a psychologist in San Francisco, uses the term "homosexualization of AIDS" to describe psychological and social processes through which identities of gay men have become entangled with the identities of those infected with HIV [1]. It is easier to overlook this phenomenon in HIV-negative men than in those who are HIV-positive because the uninfected men tend to be unknown. Mark said, "I am really afraid to tell anyone that I am HIV-negative. So many of my friends are HIV-positive that they would not want me around. I don't fit in. I can't talk about not feeling well if I am sick because they are sicker. I can't share my anxiety about having safe sex because they don't care. They would think that any problems I might have are trivial in comparison to theirs. I feel so left out. The other night I was so depressed I had a few drinks and then had unsafe sex even though I knew in the back of my mind that it is dangerous. What am I doing?"

Many gays have lived a life unaccepted by heterosexual society and now being HIV-negative frequently puts one outside one's own gay community. Because gay life has come to revolve so much around HIV, does one have to become infected in order to belong? Walt Odets, in his book, *In The Shadow of the Epidemic,* suggests that the acceptance gained by having AIDS can feel irresistible. The cost of such acceptance for the man who becomes infected is his life; but for the uninfected survivor, the entanglement of gay identity with AIDS exacts serious costs of a different, more subtle kind. Survival may be experienced as a betrayal and abandonment of those who are infected. A gay man may feel that by surviving he is betraying his personal identity as a gay person and he may feel that he is no longer part of the community [2].

Both gay/bisexual survivors who test HIV-negative and those who test HIV-positive face a myriad of issues in this pandemic. HIV-negative men may wonder why and how they remain negative when they engaged in many of the same unsafe sexual behaviors as the HIV-positive members of the community. Testing negative may give one a false sense of confidence and a belief that they must be doing something right and can therefore continue engaging in risky behavior. Being negative often creates feelings of guilt in HIV-negative men. They may also be aware of feeling isolated, as if they are the only negative person around. The numerous hospital visits and memorial services feel relentless and endless. These are constant reminders that they are well and so many others are sick. Underneath the exterior of physical health in these survivors, are hidden serious emotional problems.

For example, retesting for HIV often causes a feeling of great anxiety before and after the blood is drawn. Relief and guilt may both be present when the results are received. "How can I be happy about this," David asked me, "when so many around me are sick and dying? Of course I'm happy but I'm also very sad and confused and I feel guilty. How can I celebrate when so many are HIV-positive? I don't know where I fit anymore." Survivor guilt can manifest itself in one or all of the following:

- Mixed feelings upon learning one's HIV test results;
- Disbelief that one tested negative;
- Engaging in self-destructive behaviors which may include high-risk sexual behaviors; and
- Becoming a worried-well person frequently complaining about physical problems and looking for something to go wrong.

Even after experiencing so many conflicting feelings, many people who are HIV-negative believe that it is not OK to explore any problems they may have. It seems as if acknowledging and dealing with one's problems, would be taking something away from those who are infected. Healthy caregivers believe that their feelings don't count because, they are told, "You are healthy. Why would you have any problems?" Chris, whose life partner is infected with HIV, said, "I know I should be grateful for testing negative but I can't seem to feel OK. Because Danny is HIV-positive, I feel anxious and alone and I can't tell him how grateful I am. I think I want to attend a support group but it seems hard to find one that addresses my needs."

From 1989 to 1993 I was a co-therapist for HIV-negative gay/bisexual men's support groups in Los Angeles. Many people saw the announcements about our groups and couldn't believe them. They thought there was a mistake in the printing. They asked one man, "Why would anyone run a support group for people who are not infected?" When we asked why he thought this and called us anyway, he said "I just took a chance. I've been feeling so much guilt for being HIV-negative. Like I am the only survivor of a holocaust. I'm desperate to talk to someone before I go crazy. Are you guys for real?" We assured him that we were and when he attended a group meeting, it astonished him to meet so many other HIV-negative people looking for support. Most of those present have long believed that they are in the minority in the gay community and would never meet any else who was negative.

We advertised the groups for gay/bisexual men but we received calls from heterosexuals experiencing similar problems in relation to mixed serostatus couples. People also called with concerns about relationships and dating. These issues have become minefields of confusion and anxiety. HIV-negative survivors are worried about staying negative and have questions about safe sex. A lot of confusion still exists about what constitutes safe sex. People do not know what information they can trust. Some tend to stay in unsatisfactory relationships because the idea of meeting someone new is too scary to contemplate.

Couples of mixed HIV status—so called "serodifferent"—when one person is HIV-negative and the other, HIV-positive—need help coping as well. The usual problems couples face, like learning healthy communication and meeting individual needs, are complicated by fears of contagion, progression of the disease, and the future death of the HIV-positive partner. The partners often engage in high-risk sexual behavior since being "safe all the time feels as if we lose the intimacy we used to feel together." Ellis shared this during one of his therapy sessions. "After we did this I felt more and more anxious and really stressed out. It was really stupid but we had been growing apart lately and really needed to be together." I encouraged both men to come in for counseling to learn how to talk to each other about their needs. The impact of HIV on the relationship is strong but need not overshadow the other problems that exist. HIV can be normalized and put in its place alongside other relationship issues.

Many of the men who attended the groups came because they wanted to meet other HIV-negative men. They thought they could lessen their worries about safe sex by meeting and possibly dating another group member. Instead, they learned about the importance of personal responsibility no matter what their HIV status. Personal responsibility implies that one has found a level of comfort, for oneself, in setting safe sex guidelines in any given situation with a sexual partner. The group members talked about how feeling good enough about oneself has an impact on one's ability to make decisions during passionate moments. Personal responsibility includes acknowledging that even though one tests negative one time, any high risk sexual behavior could cause infection with HIV and subsequent seroconversion. The next testing could produce an HIV-positive result.

We spent a great deal of time discussing the nature of relationships and the development of self-esteem. Group members began to examine their previous ways of establishing relationships. What they found in the groups was other men with whom they had something in common. Gordon told us, "This is the first time I have been able to talk about what I want in a relationship without feeling uncomfortable. Everyone here understands how I feel because they have the same issues. When I talked about how concerned I was if I meet and fall in love with someone who is HIV-positive, everyone in the room nodded in agreement. Boy, did that make me feel less alone."

The fear of becoming infected by engaging in unsafe sex also raised a whole range of problems around sexuality. Many men reported increased masturbation because they were choosing to remain celibate. Some who were still dating often shared that they had problems with erections and sexual desire because of their fear of contagion and intimacy. Many people became workaholics, coming home late each day exhausted, eating a quick meal, and falling asleep with the TV on. By behaving in this manner they completely avoided the issue of dating and sexuality.

Even with all of the above mentioned issues, the majority of HIV-negative survivors feel relief and joy with their HIV status. They try to integrate their feelings of grief, sadness, and concern with goal-setting for their future or involvement in the community effort to fight the disease. They volunteer their time, become politically active or increase their monetary contributions to causes they find worthy. Building support systems where they can discuss and validate their feelings is of utmost importance and should be encouraged for the emotional health of HIV-negative people. As the need becomes more obvious, support groups for HIV-negative gay/bisexual men, women and men who are partners of HIV-positive people and anyone exploring dating and sexuality, are increasingly available. Mental health departments of AIDS service organizations often offer groups along with the ongoing individual sessions for PLWA and their caregivers.

The HIV-positive person shares many of the above concerns along with the obvious issues of his or her own health problems. Infection with HIV creates an onslaught of medical problems including tiredness, diarrhea, musculoskeletal pain, neurological problems, and in advanced cases possible blindness and dementia. The medical regimen often includes multiple medications taken throughout the day that have to be timed and coordinated with meals in order to be effective. The disease now runs one's life and the goal is to stay ahead of the various infections.

If the caregiving partner of someone with AIDS is also HIV-positive or has AIDS, the problems become more intense. Tod, a patient of mine, asked me, "What am I going to do if I become sicker? Jack is not doing very well. He had to stop working because he was constantly getting infections, and now we are trying to live on his disability check and my salary. The drugs are so expensive but we have to take them. So many of our friends are dead that we have hardly anybody to help us. I can't do so much. I'm afraid my health will suffer and I am at my wit's end." With over one million Americans infected with HIV, the number of people with medical problems will only increase. Most of these patients can be managed at home as long as possible. Community-based and in-home care programs to assist the patients and primary caregivers need to be top priorities for a health care delivery system.

The single HIV-positive person interested in dating, faces some or all of the following issues: How and when do I tell someone my HIV status? What if I meet someone and I get sicker? Will she leave me? Can I burden him with taking care of me? What can we do to make sure I do not infect her? Or make sure he doesn't re-infect me with a different strain of HIV?

Allison celebrated her twenty-first birthday at an all night bash thrown by her friends. She felt rather ill for a couple of days after and attributed her feeling that way to the partying she had done. After several weeks of not feeling better she went to the doctor. Because Allison is a recovering intravenous drug user and her symptoms were somewhat severe, the doctor tested her for HIV. The test came back positive. Allison was devastated and cried, "I can't believe this is happening to me! I've been clean for three years now and I've been using condoms. It just isn't fair. I'm young and I want to live and get married and have kids. Who is going to want me now?" Her counselors recognized the need for special interventions for her. They referred her to a support group for HIV-positive young adults where she found out that she wasn't alone. The members of the group explored ways to talk with potential partners about their condition, about safe sex and intimacy, and about planning a future. Mostly they explored their angry feelings about being cheated. They learned how to take personal responsibility for their lives and how to develop their potential for a future that had hope along with HIV.

I have spoken to many sexually active adults who refuse to be tested for HIV. They tell me that they are not in a high risk group as they still perceive gay men to be the only ones in that definition. They do not grasp the concept of high risk behaviors and are not able to let go of thinking in terms of high risk groups of people. They also share a fantasy belief that makes them certain that those to whom they are sexually attracted could not possibly be HIV-positive. "She comes from such a good family." "He looks so healthy, no way could he be HIV-positive." Comments like these are commonly heard. An HIV-infected person without AIDS may look just fine. The virus may stay hidden in the lymph nodes and other cells for many, many years.Without an HIV test, there is no way of knowing a persons' HIV status. Denial is very dangerous.

Many decide that they do not want to know their HIV status because not knowing means they do not have to worry about what to tell potential sexual partners. They believe that knowing would ruin their life. They say that they always engage in safe sex by using condoms. Knowing one's HIV status is a controversial subject and perhaps there is no one answer that is right for everyone.

The issue of personal responsibility is most important, whether one is HIV-positive, HIV-negative, or status unknown. Ongoing education related to transmission of HIV, and knowing how to protect oneself during sexual relations, are valuable tools. They help each of us know what we are willing to accept in our life in order to remain healthy while being sexually active.

REFERENCES

1. W. Odets, The Homosexualization of AIDS, *FOCUS: A Guide to AIDS Research and Counseling, 5,* October, AIDS Health Project, University of California San Francisco, 1990.
2. W. Odets, *In the Shadow of the Epidemic: Being HIV-Negative in the Age of AIDS,* Duke University Press, Durham, North Carolina, 1990.

CHAPTER 8

Needs of the Caregivers

Before and after the death of the PLWA

"The 'powerlessness' that persons in 12-step programs feel is nothing compared to that of watching friends die. I hurry around trying to help with the full realization that it is all somewhat futile." Shared by a caregiver.

As more and more people test for HIV, the issue of serostatus and its inherent problems will go beyond the gay/bisexual communities. The epidemic in the United States is spreading into populations that may be lacking formal education, have fewer financial resources, have no insurance to cover medical care, and have less ability to take control of their lives. They may be dual-diagnosed (AIDS and mental illness), homeless and/or have substance abuse problems. Finding food, clothing, and shelter take precedence over health care that is often unavailable and/or unaffordable. Violence and discrimination are prevalent among those included in these populations. It is likely that much of the stress surrounding HIV/AIDS is related to one's socioeconomic and socio-cultural status.

Social and medical needs of PLWA are becoming harder to meet as the pandemic increases and the resources decrease. Volunteer organizations and informal groups of caregivers are required to provide the patient care and support that professional caregivers can no longer handle with ease. The informal network of family and friends providing this care has become a valuable resource in the effort to provide essential services to

PLWA. These caregivers have unique needs and concerns that have to be addressed in order for the health care system to fully utilize their services. Understanding their needs and offering interventions sounds time-consuming and demanding, but in the long run, these efforts reduce professional involvement, lessen the burden for the caregiver and increase the satisfaction of the patients.

Robert Marks, editor of *FOCUS,* describes the many changes that have occurred in these volunteer networks. "Over the past few years (late 1980s, early 1990s) volunteer networks have begun to weaken, overcome by an underfunded and inaccessible health care system, and multiple loss, grief, and hopelessness. Tragically, as the health care system continues to fail, HIV-related care requires even more, the contributions of volunteer caregivers" [1, p. 2]. He goes on to describe the changing demographics of the pandemic. "When volunteer networks first developed, the gay and lesbian communities, strengthened by the political battle for recognition and by their relative affluence, were better able to take time and energy to contribute to care efforts. Injection drug users and their partners, people of color, women, and children, who comprise a greater proportion of HIV-infected people than they did in the 1980s, are often without the political and economic resources to make these contributions; the rest of society remains without the will to support people with HIV infection. The result is that none of the populations affected by HIV disease is adequately supported by the overextended volunteer networks that once served as the model for HIV-related care."

In many of the current volunteer networks, it is quite common for caregivers to be grieving the death of someone from AIDS while still continuing to be part of an informal network of family and friends caring for another person or persons with AIDS. Once again, there is a choice of whether or not to be there as a caregiver. The survivors become able to assess their strengths. They begin to realize that they know more than they ever thought one could learn about a disease. They know how to be caregivers although they may lack the skills to assess the amount of energy and availability they will need to be a caregiver once more.

As a part of the intimate involvement with a patient, caregivers learn the words to talk about the disease. Many are aware that knowing the right words to describe what is happening often relieves some of their anxiety and discomfort. Accurate information about the disease, treatment, and patient care removes some of the mystery of AIDS. It enables people to feel some control in discussions with other caregivers and makes the disease more manageable. The correct terminology makes communication clearer and tends to prevent mistakes from being made. When people use the same words and are clear on the meaning of the words, there is less chance for misinterpretations especially in regard to the care of a patient.

Many volunteers find themselves in dual roles. They may be caregivers at home or for friends as well as being part of an organization offering client support. Feelings of grief are continually stimulated and are often dealt with indirectly. Managers of organizations working with volunteers in these dual roles may better understand the behavior exhibited by their volunteers by being aware of how the process of grief is affected.

Dr. J., whose partner was dying of AIDS, was a health professional and a member of a support group for caregivers. He used his training to answer medical questions and became intensely involved with others in the group who had AIDS. His involvement in this way increased his self-esteem that was badly damaged by his inability to use his medical knowledge to save his partner.

In the grief group, Ollie became an instant caregiver to any new member. This effectively prevented him from doing his own grieving. When he became more trusting, we pointed this out to him. Only then was he able to began expressing his own feelings. He realized that withholding these feelings was a continuation of what he was forced to do in other areas of his life. In his government job, he could not express any feelings of grief that might have exposed his homosexuality.

Diseases and illnesses affect entire "families," not just the diagnosed patient. Yet, caregivers sometimes believe that any needs they have are secondary to those of the person with AIDS. These caregivers often ignore their own life stresses and concerns stating "the patient is more important" and "I should be grateful that I'm not sick." "My problems don't really count. I have to be strong." Many caregivers have told me that they feel just fine even though they are obviously exhausted. Ellen shared these thoughts, "Don needs me to be strong. I can't show him that I am not able to cope, that I need help. That would be letting him down." Nothing could be farther from the truth. If a caregiver does not take care of "self," there will be little to give to another person. Attendance at a support group for caregivers or individual sessions with a counselor can bring understanding of and support for one's needs. It is important to help caregivers learn that it is necessary to explore respite, that is, time away from caregiving. Talking with others enables caregivers to learn about resources and how to get coverage for this respite. Activities to refresh and renew can be explored. Most important of all, caregivers can learn to not feel guilty for taking care of themselves.

In "On Being a Caregiver," written for *FOCUS* in November of 1992, Denny Paterno writes about taking care of himself as he took care of his lover, Michael. "There were some activities that I found helped me to cope with the caregiving demands and the emotional issues surrounding Michael's decline. First, running and exercise provided me with time to ponder and sometimes even solve problems. This also helped to diminish the effects of stress" [2]. He spent time with Michael sharing fears and concerns of Michael's physical deterioration, eventual death, and how Denny would face life without his lover. Confronting the demons took away much of their power. Denny spent a great deal of time communicating to Michael how much Michael had given him and what the relationship meant to him. They were also very fortunate to have a wonderful skilled nursing assistant whose presence provided a feeling of security as well as an opportunity for respite. Denny remembers the difficult, scary, draining events of caregiving but mostly he recalls the depth of caring and love they were able to show each other before Michael died. Finding ways to take care of himself, allowed these feelings to be the ones most prominent after Michael's death.

Avi Rose talks about the importance of taking care of oneself. "Taking care of yourself is an essential tenet of caregiving. By the time death is imminent, many of us have already learned this lesson, but in the fray of those last days, it is important to remind yourself and to be reminded by others. Remember to eat and sleep. Get some exercise. Ask for help. Express the full range of your feelings. Be clear about priorities. Cut down on non-essential activity. Don't expect yourself to be perfect" [3]. He stresses how important it is to recognize what needs one has and then to be honest about them.

The AIDS pandemic has brought many new caregiver issues to the attention of health professionals. Being at risk for the same disease, some caregivers may be witnessing what they perceive to be their own future. This can be extraordinarily stressful. They experience fears of contamination and isolation; concerns about confidentiality, possible discrimination, the effects of homophobia; and worries about issues in the workplace. Current or former caregivers who can relate to any of these are most likely feeling additional stresses in their lives. Both the caregivers and those around them can benefit from having their concerns and stresses validated. Once accomplished, the next step is to find ways to acknowledge and cope with the reality of the strength that is needed in order to care for PLWA. Supporting this process is something a helper can offer the caregiver.

How do caregivers cope? How does one provide for the patient and provide for oneself? It is often not the future we need to explore, but rather how we coped in the past. Who was there in the past when you needed support? Who was not? How did you and your family respond to crises in the past? How are you dealing now with your own physical, emotional, social and spiritual support needs [4]? Answering these questions can bring a greater understanding of the need for a caregiving person to take care of him/herself. Recalling what gave one strength in the past to survive stressful events, will help one focus on strategies for the present.

At a point in endstage AIDS disease, the caregiver accepts that death is inevitable and sees that the physical suffering will soon be over. The caregiver will often feel relief that may be accompanied by feelings of guilt over being relieved. Guilt and relief are often accompanied by confusion, exhaustion, anger, and great distress. Realizing that these confusing and conflicting feelings are a normal and common occurrence during this period, allows people to take the first steps toward developing a support system to deal with the feelings. The need to talk to someone, to share these feelings, is very powerful. Having a support system available gives strength and courage to people allowing them to begin to be as fully present as they can be during the time preceding the death. If the caregiver is able to be present at the moment of death, the transition from life to death can have great meaning.

Because of the often intense involvement during the final illness of the deceased, it is necessary and important to recognize the loss of the caregiver role during the grieving period. It is a loss that is often overlooked and neglected. Whether the final days of the ill person were spent at home or in the hospital, the preoccupation of the caregivers is intense. They spend almost all of their time with the person who is dying. They often sleep in the same room never leaving the person's side. They fear that death will occur and they will not be there. They want to attend to every need of the patient often disregarding their own needs. The rest of their life goes by the wayside as caregiving becomes the most important thing they can do. When the death occurs, this period of intensity comes to an abrupt end. The survivor can often be found wandering aimlessly not knowing what to do. It is important for the helper to make the connection to the loss of the caregiver role that needs to be grieved along with the death and the other losses.

People thrust into the caregiver role wonder if any good can come from their sacrifices for the ones they loved. Although there is no simple answer, a member of the grief group expressed his feelings about this question. "The good that comes from being a survivor is an increased sense of having been loved and of having loved some incredible people."

REFERENCES

1. R. Marks (ed.), Editorial: The Volunteer Effort, *FOCUS: A Guide to AIDS Research and Counseling,* 7:12, November AIDS Health Project, University of California San Francisco, 1992.
2. D. Paterno, On Being a Caregiver, *FOCUS: A Guide to AIDS Research and Counseling,* 7:2, AIDS Health Project, University of California San Francisco, 1992.
3. A. Rose, HIV and Dying: The Challenges of Caring, *FOCUS: A Guide to AIDS Research and Counseling,* 11:2, January, AIDS Health Project, University of California San Francisco, 1996.
4. B. S. Wolfe, Caregivers: "Who Asks About Us?" *Grief Notes, 12*:2, A Publication of St. Mary's Grief Support Center, Duluth, Minnesota, 1997.

CHAPTER 9

Dealing with Death in the Workplace

Eventually the bereaved person is able to concentrate more on the world around him. Each person begins to find his or her own rhythm. The healing process is occurring, the feelings come and go and there is the realization that life goes on. Those survivors of AIDS deaths who return to the workplace may encounter difficulties adjusting and being accepted because of the stigma attached to HIV/AIDS.

Brad said, "I took some time off work while Dan was sick and went back a few weeks after his funeral. I wanted to get on with my life. Some of my co-workers had come to the memorial service, but when I got to my desk that first day, no one said anything. It was like some big secret and it felt as if they were all uncomfortable in my presence and didn't know what to say or do." He worked for a fairly conservative company and was worried about losing his job if they knew that he was gay. He had only come out to some of his closest co-workers. Brad choose not to be more open about his sexual orientation because he remembered when a friend lost a job because he was "outed" after a lover died of AIDS-related illness. Thus, Brad was aware of the loss of potential support from many of those with whom he worked.

Brad's story is fairly common. People either don't know what to say or they mumble words such as "I'm sorry" or "How are you doing?" and continue working. Not too many want to talk about the death. Everyone becomes engrossed in their job and effectively avoids the mourner. Brad shared with me that he wasn't looking for a lot of attention but he did want people to acknowledge the importance of his loss. He noticed that after this death from AIDS, the discomfort of his co-workers was deeper and their avoidance of him greater than when deaths occurred from other conditions.

There are effective ways to welcome the griever back into his or her work routine. The wise employer knows that continuing employment can restore the confidence and self-esteem that are often lost during difficult, stressful times. The standards set by a manager will give employees a sense of acceptance, security, and value for their feelings. In turn, people in this type of environment put their best efforts into the work they do. An accepting, supportive environment can be created and employers who are sensitive to life crises, including the need to grieve, can maintain productivity in the work place. Each employer has to explore his or her policies in regard to level of involvement with the survivor, flexibility of work schedules, time-off for bereavement, and provision of support for all employees. Grief work is often difficult and lonely but it can be eased by an environment that is welcoming to the process.

AARP (American Association of Retired Persons) [1], National Funeral Directors Association [2], and the American Hospice Foundation [3] publish pamphlets that describe steps employers can take to better assist bereaved employees. Included are the following suggestions:

- Inquire directly about an employee's loss. The wrong thing is to say nothing.
- Offer specific help with work or home tasks.
- Listen without judgments if employees want to share their feelings. When appropriate, share experiences and feelings avoiding comparisons.
- Be open to negotiating time off during the first year of bereavement.
- Suggest ways to maintain productivity such as organizing tasks or temporarily reassigning jobs.
- Suggest counseling or support groups.
- Obtain print resources like pamphlets, or arrange bereavement workshops to increase sensitivity of employees to the issues of grief.

- Expect to hear the story many times because sharing is part of the healing. Set limits and, if need be, offer to continue the discussion at another time.
- Recognize that confidentiality can become an issue for managers hearing their employees' stories and reactions to grief.

It is important for the employer and/or manager to keep in touch with other employees during this period of time who may be feeling their own grief and may cry or be emotional. This is a good time to encourage mutual support and teamwork. The following suggestions may be helpful:

- Acknowledge that the impact of their losses is recognized and provide quiet moments and closed doors.
- Be sure to include the grieving employee in office social events. It may be helpful to someone who is feeling isolated.
- Thank the staff for sharing the emotional burden and the extra work.
- Support the efforts of all who help the mourner.
- Expect the best but accept less for a while.

The bereaved person, likewise, has to be proactive in understanding his or her needs. It is wise to talk to the employer about bereavement leave policy, work hours, resources for grief support, a private place to have quiet time when needed, and respect for confidentiality. Although people mean well, they may appear to be insensitive. Co-workers may be as inexperienced in grief matters as the mourner and understanding and working together is most important. The grief of the survivor will cause co-workers to relive their own loss experience and they may want to share their stories and pain. This could be helpful and mutually supportive or could be unbearable. In any case, it is important for all to be as clear as possible about what their own needs are and how they can get them met.

Another workplace situation needs recognition here—the death of a co-worker. The above suggestions all apply and are important. The manner in which the loss is experienced depends on the relationship each person had with the deceased.

In addition, employee grief is affected by the way the person died, the size of the company, the interaction of all employees, the type of job done by the deceased and the attitude of the employer. The American Hospice Foundation offers some suggestions for handling grief at work:

- Be sensitive to the wishes of the survivors and to those of the deceased (if known) in regard to disclosing the cause of death.
- Call an informal meeting of the employees where permission is given to grieve and talk about feelings.
- Ask a trained grief counselor to meet and talk with the staff, if needed.
- Advise employees of the time and date of any funeral arrangements and/or memorial service and offer them time off to attend.
- Find a way to honor the person who died. Money could be collected for a charitable donation or scholarship fund. A tribute could be placed in a company newsletter and a memorial book or bulletin board could be compiled [3].

AIDS service organizations are among the most affected of all workplaces. Their employees are confronted with losses on all levels. Their clients are living with, and dying from, AIDS. Since many of the employees are members of an affected community, their lovers, friends, and colleagues are infected with and affected by HIV. Many of these employees are themselves infected with HIV and are struggling with their own health issues. Administrators of some of these agencies are just now recognizing the need to offer grief and loss support groups for their staff.

Much of the so-called "burnout" and turnover in AIDS service organizations is due to the lack of attention paid to employee grief and mourning. Unresolved grief causes additional stress in these already over-stressed organizations. Problems such as reduced productivity, low morale, increased conflict, absenteeism, difficulty setting limits, and inadequate attention to positive feedback and informal support are often found in the workplace [4].

Within AIDS service organizations, if employees feel that it is unsafe or unprofessional to discuss personal AIDS grief, it will be hard to get rid of burnout or turnover problems. In the workplace, management needs to support these difficult employee discussions about feelings of grief. Employees given an opportunity to express their feelings in a safe support group, are able to return to their demanding work feeling more validated. Having a place to talk with other colleagues experiencing the enormous losses is very valuable. It allows them to feel less isolated from their co-workers. Feeling connected and understood allows them to increase their productivity with the clients they are serving.

Caesar M., an in-home health case worker, related, "When I hear Margo talking in group about all the clients she had who died, I can really feel her pain. It makes it OK for me to say how much my clients meant to me and how helpless I feel a lot of the time. I can return to my desk knowing that I can talk to her or other group members during the day if I need to."

The recognition that death is a part of life in the workplace as well as in the rest of the life of the mourner helps toward a healthy resolution of grief. When one is allowed to appropriately incorporate the grief into other activities, a sense of balance can be restored more easily. Valuing feelings supports the need for people to reorganize their life and find new directions for themselves.

REFERENCES

1. American Association of Retired Persons (AARP), When an Employee Loses a Loved One, It Pays to Take Time to Care, *Social Outreach and Support Programs Division Pamphlet*, Washington, D.C., 1991.
2. National Funeral Directors Association, Inc., Co-Worker Death, *Pamphlet*, 11121 West Oklahoma Avenue, Milwaukee, Wisconsin 53227-4096, 1995.
3. J. Turner, Grief at Work: A Guide for Employees and Managers, *Pamphlet*, American Hospice Foundation, Washington, D.C., 1995.
4. K. Schoen, Managing Grief in AIDS Organizations, *FOCUS: A Guide to AIDS Research and Counseling*, 7:6, May, AIDS Health Project, University of California San Francisco, 1992.

CHAPTER 10

The Language of Death and Dying

The words we use, the things we say

There is no escape from the fact that many societies are uncomfortable with the expressed words, behaviors, and feelings of grief. Death language (terminology) is very powerful and is used or avoided in a unique way in each society. In the United States the use of descriptive words like dead, died, death, and dying is almost nonexistent when we discuss someone who has died. We refer to that occurrence using language omitting the word or words that best describe what happened.

Instead, we often hear survivors talking about the "passage" of their loved one: "He or she passed away," "passed on," or "passed over;" "departed" or "made the transition." People often say, "he bought the farm," "she croaked," "he kicked the bucket," or "he caught the last train." People even "expire" like an outdated medication.

Words related to death are often used in a context totally unrelated to the circumstance. You might hear a friend say, "I was dying to read that book." Partygoers talking the day after an event might say, "You should have seen him, he was 'dead drunk' last night." Leaving a class after finals you might hear, "Boy, that exam was deadly." We also hear sentences similar to these; "I was bored to death at that party," or "She was dead tired after the California AIDS Bike Ride."

In Nora Ephron's novel *Heartburn,* a nurse pulls the sheet over a woman's face. She exclaims "Mother's gone." Mother, however, whips off the sheet and then faints. The startled nurse says, "Fainted dead away." "This goes to show an anomaly of hospital life," says Ephron, "which is that they only use the word 'dead' when it doesn't apply" [1].

When I teach about death and dying, I ask participants to shout out the words death, dead, dying, and deceased. At first they can't do it. They feel uncomfortable and self-conscious. Some tend to whisper, if indeed, they are able to utter any words. There is much laughter and shuffling around.

Only after repeatedly shouting out the words are they able to desensitize themselves and continue with a discussion of the reasons for their difficulty. When I ask why it seems so hard to say "She died," some answer that it is difficult because it shows a lack of respect for the deceased. Others say it is too blunt. They believe that the mourners (and perhaps themselves) would be shocked by the direct use of "those words."

The class participants suggest that we should couch the language with more sensitivity. What they mean is that avoiding the use of descriptive words makes people appear to be more sensitive. By *not* using accurate words, people can push away some of the uncomfortable feelings that arise around death. It is difficult to accept that speaking the words also increases our own feelings of vulnerability and discomfort. When we hear the words we become more aware of our own mortality. This can be too painful and we want to avoid the discomfort. Not using accurate death language can sometimes produce both humorous and disturbing or confusing miscommunications. For example: Miriam and Linda, old friends who hadn't seen each other in a while, met at the store. Miriam said to Linda, "My husband is gone." Linda responded, "Mine is gone too." "When did Alex die?" asked Miriam. "Oh, Alex didn't die," answered Linda. "We're divorced."

This example illustrates the common use of words such as "gone" instead of "died" and the confusion that ensues. Michael Ventura writes in the *Los Angeles Weekly* of 10/13/92, " 'Gone' is more ambivalent, and matches the ambivalence we're left with after a loved one's death. Because an absence isn't just something in the past, something finished. An absence happens in the present, and, if it's an important absence, it can function as a kind of presence—a presence in which qualities are highlighted that were taken for granted, or not realized at all; other qualities are forgotten; and even what one thought one knew is seen differently in the light of absence" [2].

Words like death, dead or died are so final sounding yet are comforting to some people. Bereaved persons may be comfortable using these words when people who offer condolences also feel comfortable using them. The use of specific death language tells the mourners that their visitors are with them in the experience. Hearing these words may help them feel less alone.

To others, the finality of the words is too unsettling. Hearing accurate language means that the person *really* has died. Even though this is the case, we often guard against coming right out and saying so at a time soon after the death. We may feel protective of the mourners and want to allow them to accept the finality of death when they are ready. When the mourner hears, "I feel so sad that your Father died," it might be experienced as too much of a shock. Perhaps there is less trauma if the mourner hears "I'm so sorry about your Father." Or, "I am sorry for your loss." This becomes confusing as we want to use correct language to be direct yet we want to protect the person who is hurting.

When we are with the mourners immediately following the death, we may want to use more descriptive words. However, a more gentle approach might be best. As more time goes by after the death, it may feel more acceptable to use accurate words such as "death" and "died."

Mourners tend to feel and act differently during each of the ongoing phases of the grief process. As their feelings and actions change over time, their needs will also change. Listening to the language used by the mourner can guide one's choice of words. If the grieving person initiates the use of specific death language, he or she will be ready to hear it from the visitor. When the visitor is comfortable with the remarks made, visits with the mourner tend to be more comforting. When our goal is to be a helper, the secret is finding out if the person feels helped.

At all times, it is important to understand one's motivation in choosing language to speak about death. The question to ask is, "What is important to convey at each moment? Chances are that you sincerely want to acknowledge the pain and loss of the survivor. Doing so decreases the chance that he or she will feel abandoned. A feeling of abandonment is often a result of people not responding in some way to the death because they do not know what to say or do.

People might find themselves avoiding a condolence call thinking that they will say something wrong. They are afraid that they might make the grief worse by calling attention to the death (as if the survivors aren't already thinking about it all the time). Staying away sets up a problem at a time when no one wants to create more pain for the mourner or guilt for themselves. The grieving person often feels like a pariah and avoidance by friends and family intensifies their anguish. On the other hand, the need to be alone can be quite important for the survivor. It is therefore necessary to ask when a visit will be welcome.

There are times when people think it would be best to pay respects to the mourner even if they did not care for the deceased. They may not even feel sad. In these situations they want to be polite and not sound insincere. Regardless of their thoughts about the deceased, speaking ill of the dead is not an option. People can choose ways to express their sympathy to the mourner without saying anything about the deceased. "I am sorry about your loss," will acknowledge the mourners' feelings and will be truer than "I'm sorry that Joe died."

So we often find ourselves trying to build a repertoire of words and sayings that we can use when paying a condolence call. Developing this repertoire is difficult because the language of death makes many of us so uncomfortable. Instead, the mourner often hears well-meaning family, friends, and acquaintances utter comments that he or she perceive as insensitive, unhelpful, and even stupid.

The following section describes some of these words and sentences. Inappropriate comments cause mourners to feel irritated, angry, and even enraged.

I know exactly how you are feeling.

I can imagine how you are feeling.

I understand how you are feeling.

We truly cannot know another person's experience. "People don't understand," Jake, a patient of mine, complained. A friend of his shared that her daughter had died in an auto accident. The daughter was the same age as Jake's lover was when he died. Jake's friend said she understood his grief. Jake confronted his friend with, "At least you didn't have to watch your daughter suffer. So how *could* you understand."

I'm always here for you, call me if you need something.

Making an open-ended statement like the one above sounds like a caring offer. However, the mourners are put at a disadvantage since they are not certain that the comment is sincere. They will rarely call for assistance. If people really want to be helpful, they must be sure to make a more definitive statement about their availability.

You should be over it by now. It's time you moved on.

A patient of mine came in for her session visibly upset and very angry. When I inquired why she was feeling this way, she told me she had just spoken to a close friend of hers. The friend had called to invite my patient, Gale, to a party. Gale, whose daughter died six months ago, said to this friend, "I'm not ready yet to go to a party." Her friend replied, "It's over six months already. Time to be over it. It's time you got back into life."

Telling people that they "should be over it" implies that grieving is unbecoming. Comments similar to this can cause the mourner to become enraged with the speaker and embarrassed or ashamed at his or her own behavior. Under circumstances like this, the grieving person begins to withdraw from the speaker and/or withhold outward signs of grief. Internalizing the grief reactions by withholding them almost always creates physical distress. One consequence of holding in feelings is made clear by this quote. "The sorrow that has no vent in tears makes other organs weep" (author unknown).

In actuality, the observer is most likely feeling discomfort with the mourner's expression of grief. Seeing pain expressed with tears, and often, wailing, is too difficult to watch and friends want it to stop. They do not want to "break" the mourner by allowing tears to continue. Most of all, they want to protect themselves from the feelings these actions bring up in them.

Living in a culture that doesn't promote the expression of feelings, makes people protect themselves from becoming vulnerable. When the show of feelings brings comments from observers telling one to stop, the pain of the grief coupled with the lack of understanding will be too intense for some mourners to continue being vulnerable. At the same time it is often hard to distinguish if the pain of the mourners is for the loss of the deceased or for themselves as the one experiencing the loss, or for both.

You had so many years together. You are so lucky.

When a well-meaning friend of a patient of mine whose husband had just died said to her "You had so many years together." My patient reported thinking, "What about growing older together? What about our hopes and dreams? We had plans for the future, things we wanted to do. Now all that has been taken away. I really miss what could have been."

The following statements and others like them show great insensitivity to the mourner and to his or her relationship with the loved one who died. Survivors feel rage and great pain when they hear comments like these:

At least you have other children.

You're young, you'll meet someone else.

At least her suffering is over. She is in a better place now.

He lived a really long and full life.

How old was he?

Why do some people ask how old the deceased was? Should an older person's death be less painful because he or she lived longer? Asking only about the age of the deceased totally disregards the value of that person in the life of the survivor. This survivor may hear that his or her pain should be less intense than that experienced by others because the deceased was old.

It seems that those who are grieving the death of a young person receive more sympathy than those whose loved one died at an older age. Comments like "children aren't supposed to die before their parents" or "he or she didn't fulfill his or her potential" are quite commonly said as though they offer comfort. People may be trying to show that they are on the same wavelength and understand the mourners' thoughts about the death. Yet, most survivors do not feel comforted or understood when they hear these remarks.

Questions about age are especially poignant in AIDS-related deaths where those who are dying are often under forty years of age. People often comment on the fact that the deceased didn't reach their potential because he or she died so young. Who among us really knows what someone's potential is meant to be? Focusing on this aspect of someone's life creates more stress and anxiety for the mourner. It is often more helpful to talk about the accomplishments of the one who died than to fantasize about what might have been.

> When my cousin died, my aunt was really devastated. I'll bet you are too.

Comments like this to the mourner imply comparison. It doesn't help to compare the grief to anything or anyone else. The bereaved then feels confused about whether to express his or her own pain and grief or to explain why this is or isn't true. The attention moves away from the mourner creating an awkward moment for everyone.

Contrast the above remarks with the following comments found to be helpful by people who are grieving.

> I am sorry that you are going through this painful experience.

It must be hard to accept that this has happened.

It's OK to grieve and be really angry with God and anyone else.

I did not know _____, will you tell me about him? What was your relationship like?

Asking about the deceased in this manner is especially helpful if you did not know the person who died but want to pay your respects to the survivor. Talking about their loved one helps them on their journey toward resolution. Be prepared to use the name of the deceased when talking about the death. By so doing, you recognize that he or she was a part of life at one time and can continue to be a part of the survivor's life, only now in a different way.

The husband of an art collector was devastated by the death of his wife. He came to the next showing of an artist whose works she collected, to talk about his wife and her love of those pieces. The artist had also been a personal friend and was more than willing to share memories. The husband felt very close to his wife during this sharing and left feeling more peaceful and resolved about her death.

When thinking about how to offer comfort, it is acceptable to ask questions that invite mourners to discuss how they feel. One should enter into this type of dialogue only if willing and able to hear the mourner's response. One's interest in talking about the death can be acknowledged by sharing stories, tears, and memories. The depth of every loss is very personal and willingness to share conveys respect for the emotional attachment of the survivor to the deceased.

Florence knew that the "right thing" to do was to ask Norm about the death of his partner. She was afraid that she would upset him but she finally got up enough courage to approach him. "I'm so sorry that Lee died, Norm. I wish I could have been at the funeral. Will you tell me about the service you had?" Norm opened up to her and shared how beautiful it was and how many people were there and how peaceful Lee looked and on and on. He told her how relieved he was to be able to talk about the funeral and how much it meant to him that she had asked. He said that most people avoided talking about Lee and he really wanted to share what had happened.

Many people live much of their lives in an environment where feelings are not discussed. When a death occurs, they may find themselves surrounded by people sharing intense feelings. This may be difficult and uncomfortable for them. Pressures may be created for them to conform to the situation without their having the skills to do so. People may not realize that they have options such as excusing themselves for the moment if the situation becomes too intense. One such situation is a post-funeral gathering. Talk of the deceased may increase feelings of discomfort and create many awkward moments. It is quite all right to find something to do like straightening up or helping in the kitchen if one needs to escape the intensity of feelings.

The first few weeks following a death is a difficult time with business to take care of and a lot of contact with family and friends. After this initial period of intense activity, mourners are often left alone. This is a good time to invite the mourner to take a walk, to go on a quiet outing or to spend time in a way the mourner chooses.

> I can bring dinner over either Tuesday or Friday. Which will be better for you?

Grief is stressful and it is of the utmost importance for people who are grieving to eat healthy meals. At the same time, they have neither the interest nor the energy to prepare food properly. Many studies document immune system compromise after a loss. If nutrition is not managed, likelihood of illness is higher. The offer to deliver meals (with lots for leftovers) will be appreciated. It is best for people to say when they can do this. Giving the recipient a choice of times and days shows true intent.

> I can run some errands for you in the morning. Would that be helpful to you?

Before contacting a mourner, a helper must decide how much time is available in his schedule to spend with the person who is grieving. It is OK to make personal choices about the level of involvement. If one is clear about limits, it will be easier to connect. These choices can be shared with the mourner and, together, a plan can be chosen. Mourners may be grieving but they are not usually helpless or incapable of making decisions.

Being with someone who is grieving offers a choice to say nothing or very little. Just being there quietly can be a great comfort. We don't think of "just being there" as "doing something." We think we always have to be active in our support. Being there *is* doing something. We only have to learn how to see "action" in a different light.

No matter how much people learn about ways of talking to a mourner in person, if they are not comfortable with their word choices, the mourner will experience the speaker's distress. Under these circumstances solace will be limited. Writing a note is another form of communicating your condolences. Putting the words on paper enables people to use death-specific words that they are unable to say in person. It is often easier for people to read words like death, died, and dead than to hear them aloud.

Signing ones' name to store-bought condolence cards is an option many choose. People often add a short note that includes the deceased's name. Personalizing the note in this way creates an opportunity to include thoughts, fond memories and/or a humorous story about the person who died.The sender can also read these pre-written cards to get ideas to incorporate into his or her own notes. A heartfelt note allows people to include a part of themselves in their expression of sympathy.

Cards and notes are tangible evidence from someone who cares. The survivor appreciates the thought and will have the cards available at any time to savor and treasure. Specific words in the notes tell the mourner that support is available. These cards give them something to hold and reread at the loneliest of times.

The death of a loved one often devastates the survivors. The way along the path to resolution is complicated by the inability to use words like dead, died, and death. But the caring responses offered during bereavement ease the grief. Respectful support from friends and family enables mourners to become aware of, understand and eventually accept the anger, guilt, confusion, helplessness, and deep sadness that is a consequence of their loss.

The use of specific death language mirrors people's own comfort level for feeling the intensity of the pain surrounding death. As people experiment with the use of these specific words, they may become more in touch with their level of death awareness. Being in close contact with death can raise issues of one's own mortality and create opportunities for the exploration of one's feelings about death. As people increase their comfort with specific death language they also increase their familiarity with the range of thoughts and feelings that accompany loss. In this process they begin to prepare themselves for the inevitable experiences of loss and death that occur in all of our lives.

THE LANGUAGE OF DEATH AND DYING

- Feeling comfortable using accurate death language such as dead, died, and death will be helpful to the mourners and to those who wish to be supporters.

- When offering condolences, it is helpful to the mourner to hear the name of the deceased. Sharing thoughts and memories of the one who died is another way to offer comfort.

- Know the type of support and assistance one is comfortable offering the mourner and be specific about the offer.

- Notes and cards enable people to express thoughts and feelings that they may be uncomfortable saying in person.

- Receiving a note and/or a sympathy card gives mourners something tangible to read and hold on to when times are hard.

REFERENCES

1. N. Ephron, *Heartburn,* Random House, Inc., New York, 1983.
2. M. Ventura, Editorial, *Los Angeles Weekly,* Los Angeles, California, October 13, 1992.

CHAPTER 11

Cultural Dimensions of Grief

Why it is important to understand the differences

Our own feelings, around grief and the death of our loved ones, are impacted by cultural, ethnic, religious and spiritual rituals, and beliefs. This chapter offers a brief discussion about the beliefs of various cultures. Being in touch with cultural values around death and dying can offer comfort and direction during a very difficult period of time.

In the best of circumstances, there will be occasions for the person who is dying to express his or her needs and expectations about death, funeral arrangements, and memorial services to those close to him, to those who have the power to carry out his or her wishes. But, the best scenario is not always the one that occurs. Perhaps the person who is dying is unable to accept his pending death. He may not be able to initiate a discussion fearing that those around him may not be able to hear his needs or that he will worry them too much. The family members may want to handle the after death arrangements their own way without regard to the desires of the person who is dying. They may be reluctant to bring up the topic believing that it may make the ill person feel worse. Whenever possible, it is valuable to talk with persons who are dying about what they want to happen to them after death. Sharing their experiences of other deaths and funerals; and their fears and fantasies about dying, death and afterlife, help all to prepare for the events that will soon occur.

Here are some suggestions for facilitating the often difficult discussions about death arrangements and wishes with people who are aware that their condition is imminently life threatening. Approach the person when there will be quiet time to explore the issues; choose a time free of interruptions such as meals or taking medications. Begin the conversation in this way. "This may be as difficult for you as it is for me but I think we need to talk about your final wishes. I want to make sure that I can take care of whatever you want. I want to understand the religious or spiritual beliefs you have so they can be incorporated in any service we do. Will you be willing to share this information with me now? Do you want anyone else to be present? Is it OK for me to write this all down?"

A therapist, Nancy, whom I supervised, had a client, Lily, who was nearing the end of her life. Nancy was feeling anxious about listening to Lily talk about her coming death. We discussed these anxieties and found out that Nancy was afraid of Lily becoming emotional, agitated, or angry. I encouraged the therapist to approach Lily in a gentle, open manner. She agreed to try to do this. When she initiated the conversation, Lily did start to cry but for a different reason than anticipated. Lily said, "I am so grateful that you were willing to discuss this with me. Since I got AIDS everyone avoids me. I know I am dying and I do have some wishes. I am really worried about my kids and I want to make arrangements for them to be cared for. I think I have to put it in writing with a lawyer or somebody, don't I?" Nancy told her that would be the best way to insure that the children would be placed where she wanted them. Nancy helped Lily make an appointment with an attorney to come to her bedside to complete the necessary paperwork. Lily made arrangements to place her son and daughter with some relatives in a nearby city and was finally at peace in this matter.

Lily began talking about her childhood experiences in church and requested that Nancy ask a former minister of hers to come and visit so she could explain what kind of funeral service she wanted. Both Lily and the therapist, Nancy, felt good about the interaction that ultimately set up a plan for the children and for Lily's funeral.

There is always the chance that someone approaching a dying person will hear the response I got from Simon. "Just cremate me and forget everything else," he told me angrily. "I don't believe in God or religion or afterlife. I don't want a bunch of people crying and carrying on over me." I told him that I was glad he was so clear about what he wanted and that he needed to make sure he put all of that in writing. I said I would help him. I then asked him the following question, "Do you have any suggestions for how your friends could honor their relationship with you? I have seen several of them visiting you on a regular basis and I believe they will want to do something. What would be acceptable to you?" Simon said reluctantly and defiantly, "Well, I guess they could all go to Mickey's at our regular time on a Friday night and dance a couple of dances while they remember what fun we used to have."

As people near death, they sometimes return for comfort to rituals long ignored while they lived their lives. James and his lover shared an active "new age" spiritual life for the twelve years of their relationship. James was quite taken aback when Jon asked him to find a Catholic priest to perform his last rites. Neither James nor Jon realized that as death approached, renewing his early Catholic connections would enable Jon to feel more at peace.

Before he died, Sam told his lover, Kenneth, that even though his parents did not accept his homosexuality, he knew that their grief would be intense and that they would use Jewish rituals to help them deal with their grief. Sam explained some of the possible rituals Kenneth would see at the funeral. Because he knew what to expect, Kenneth was able to understand why Sam's parents insisted that the funeral happen as soon as possible. He also understood why they chose a simple wooden casket, and why, as the casket was lowered into the ground, anyone who wanted to could approach to shovel dirt into the grave. Knowing the role these rituals played in the parents lives, allowed Kenneth to avoid interpreting them as a rejection of him.

Sam's parents were aware of the loving bond between the two men even though they were not accepting of the relationship. Their love for their son and their desire to fulfill his wishes after his death allowed them to reach out to Kenneth in a small way. They made suggestions for his participation that would be religiously appropriate and he chose a poem to read during the service. Meeting each other this way allowed the mourners to interact in a caring fashion that honored the deceased and his love for all of them.

Not all parents are so understanding and many of them blame the surviving partner for the death of their child. Susan and Joseph shared with me their struggle over their son Delane's death and funeral service. "We know that Delane wasn't involved with our church anymore since he and Dennis were together and that really hurt us. We didn't raise him that way. He told us we could do whatever we wanted when he died because he'd be dead and wouldn't care anymore. We wanted to follow our tradition so we could ease our hearts, but it felt like Delane wasn't part of our life anymore. Like we didn't even know him. Dennis wanted to be part of the service, but we just couldn't accept that. He caused our son's death. They had their own life and we want him out of ours. Dennis would just have to deal with that himself."

Because Salvador's family had insisted on taking the body back to Guatemala, his life partner, Jason, and his friends in Los Angeles, wondered how they would be able to have a funeral service to remember Sal. They finally decided to approach the minister of the church to which they belonged to explore possibilities. The minister suggested that they set a date for a memorial service in the church. He asked them to enlarge a picture of Salvador, record his favorite music on one tape and bring some of his favorite belongings. The friends also decided to ask people to speak about Sal at the service. They couldn't believe how many accepted. People wrote out their thoughts, feelings and experiences and presented them to Jason in a scrapbook for him to refer to any time he wanted to remember Sal and feel close to him. Everyone agreed that this was a wonderful, fitting memorial to this much loved man and that his spirit was with them even if his body was not.

Diverse cultures in the United States are often based on race, ethnicity, or shared social behaviors similar to that in the gay and lesbian community. Without an adequate understanding of the attitudes, values, and beliefs of different cultures, sensitivity for the individual needs of the mourners cannot be realized [1]. Those who are HIV-infected or have AIDS are reflected in this cultural diversity, but the stigma surrounding them often prevents people from remaining connected to their cultural roots. Feeling unaccepted, they frequently leave homes and neighborhoods and move into more assimilated environments. After death, some families come to claim the body and return with it to their homes. These families often have to lie about the cause of death in order to participate in cultural rituals and to have a proper burial for the deceased. Along with feelings of guilt for keeping the truth secret, the survivor is also left with a conflicted feeling for betraying the life of the deceased. Many gay men have been buried "straight" because of their families' discomfort with the truth of who they were and how they died.

Supporters or helpers are encouraged to explore cultural differences with people who are grieving the death of someone from AIDS who come to them for counseling. Open discussions will be beneficial to all. The mourners will be able to distinguish between that which is part of their culture and that which is connected to their personal experiences surrounding the death of their loved one(s). Misunderstandings and mistrust of the health care system may have been part of the experience of caregiving during the final illness. Therefore, validation of sexual and ethnic differences after the death can help alleviate the mourner's confusion during the time of intense grief. People differ in their relationships with others, in their understanding of loss, in the way they externalize feelings and in their willingness be a part of the customs related to death. There is, however, usually a common denominator, which is to console the survivor.

While Phil was in the hospital, Enrique's family came in great numbers to help care for both the men. They brought food and meaningful objects from home to comfort Phil. They would gather in the halls and pray. An insensitive nursing staff continually told the family members that they were in the way or were making too much noise. They were asked to leave the hospital. Phil and Enrique found the family support welcome and this insensitivity increased the anxiety they felt. The situation caused great distress for all concerned. After Phil died, many family members wanted to sue the hospital and ventilate their anger at the nursing staff. One of the cousins could see that Enrique was becoming increasingly agitated and she called a meeting of the family. "Our most important concern now is to take care of Enrique. He has suffered enough and we have to offer him some peace and support. Maybe later he will talk to the hospital administration, but now he needs us to be there for him." Validation and understanding can help the mourner reconnect with his traditions and belief systems and enable him to participate in rituals he finds meaningful.

Helpers need to not make assumptions about the rituals engaged in by each person. More specific information about their needs can be gotten by asking non-judgmental questions of the mourner. Theories and techniques should not be presented blindly. Openness to the survivors different beliefs should be a top priority. Ask the survivors how their families handled grief. Ask them to share their experiences with death in the community where they live. People of different cultures and ethnic groups may not value approaches to grief counseling that encourage expressing emotions, verbalizing their thoughts, maintaining eye contact, gaining insight, focusing on long-term goals or distinguishing between physical and mental health. It is important to know what is valued in expressions of grief.

Caucasian experiences are influenced by individual religious and/or spiritual involvement, tradition and beliefs as well as a family's country of origin. What is important is not to make assumptions about ones needs and desires but to ask questions and gather information to meet the needs of the deceased and of the mourners. The Fairfax County, VA Department of Human Development presented a workshop on *Crisis Intervention for Child Fatalities* and in the workshop manual they described the following diverse cultural rituals [2]. These general statements are presented here to increase awareness and to offer guidelines for exploration of the differences among people. Even though feelings of grief are common to all peoples, the way different cultures deal with grief is not a shared human behavior. People will respond differently and will require different approaches to encourage the healing of survivors. Acculturation gives us an introduction to the behavior of others and mourners may want to integrate other ideas into their own beliefs. Integrating new ideas may prove to be difficult since detaching from ones traditional beliefs can create distance within a family that will deprive the griever of much needed support. Starting and sharing new traditions, however, can bring people closer together.

Although the following discussion presents certain specific experiences, many of the traditions and rituals of the different cultures and religions overlap and seem similar. Others are known only to a particular population.

The *African American* experience is described as generally including the belief that one goes to God looking their best. There is a belief that ancestors protect the living. Everyone in the community may be included as "extended family" and is expected to come to the funeral. There will be much singing, wailing, crying, and even fainting. Flowers are placed on the grave on holidays as well as on the anniversary of the death and at other visits. Survivors need to stay connected to the deceased so it is not helpful to encourage them to "let them go" or to "get on with your life." Differences will exist between groups of African Americans based on communication styles, cross-cultural experiences, skin color, country of origin, and socioeconomic class.

There is devotion shown to the deceased and the body is treated well in many cultures. *Hispanic and Latino Americans* hold this belief and place great importance on family unity and loyalty. They believe that it is important for the body to be returned to its birth country. Friends and relatives will chip in if the family does not have enough money. Relatives are expected to show outward expression of their emotions and funerals are seen as social events, not unlike weddings or baptisms. The Catholic church is seen as a tremendous resource and a location to receive ongoing support.

Americans of *Middle Eastern* origins, depending upon their religious traditions, tend not to believe in pre-arrangements, such as buying a grave site in advance. The deceased can be buried in the community in which he lived and it is an obligation for neighbors to attend the funeral. The body is washed and covered with sheets within forty-eight hours either by the family or by community volunteers. It is believed that if the deceased was good, he or she passed into a better world. There is a three-day mourning period, sometimes extending to one year. As a helper, it is important to know that a person of the opposite sex should not be touched, that there be no open talk about sex, and that prolonged eye contact with the mourner is to be avoided.

In the *Korean American* culture the person is often brought home to die. If possible, the dying person will verbalize a will and all those present witness the dying person's desires. Mourners will cry loudly so the whole neighborhood will hear that the person has died. Burial will be on an odd numbered day as that means "bright" as opposed to even numbered days connoting "shadowy." Grief lasts for three years with up to five generations participating in the grieving process. There are rituals surrounding the grief process on the first and the fifteenth day of the month that include displaying a picture of the deceased, serving the favorite foods and lighting a candle. After three years, the display is set up once a year.

Asian-Pacific Americans comprise over twenty different groups and each group may speak a different language and have a different religion. Helpers should be aware that discussion or disclosure of feelings with strangers may not be accepted in this culture.

Vietnamese-Americans believe that color is very important at the funeral ceremony, and thus no black is worn. White is the color of choice with other colors denoting certain relationships to the deceased. The mourning period is also three years during which time there are no marriages, no high fashion worn and no new hair styles.

Customs of the *Jewish* religion include showing great respect for life and this respect continues for the deceased. A guardian is required to remain with the body until the burial. The funeral service honors the person who died by having a summary of the value of his life and the good deeds performed. A one-year mourning period is divided into stages beginning with the moment of death. The first seven days following the funeral are meant for comforting the mourners after which they are encouraged to slowly rejoin society. Consolation is offered by reaffirming life. The deceased person is remembered by the tradition of lighting a special tall candle in a glass that, when lit, burns for seven days from the day of the funeral. It should be in plain sight as a sign that the family is mourning. As a memorial, a "Yahrtzeit" candle is lit once a year on the anniversary of the death and it burns for twenty-four hours.

Buddhists prepare the deceased for reincarnation on the forty-ninth day following the death. Perhaps someone observing certain behaviors related to reincarnation, i.e., seemingly inappropriate joy at the death, may see these behaviors as weird and disrespectful. Finding out that the belief for this expression of joy is related to the fact that the deceased is now nearer to his creator and that spending time on earth was just a means to a wonderful end, allows one to understand and to be more accepting to the response to death in a culture such as this.

Rituals can be comforting even if the mourners do not accept them in their totality. Relating to a certain part of a tradition as opposed to the whole belief system, can still offer comfort and solace. Perhaps some mourners will want to recognize the death with a combination of rituals taken from different cultures that become integrated into one new tradition.

The gay communities, so hard hit by the AIDS pandemic, have developed a meaningful tradition with rituals that are unique to them. Memorial services are redefined as "Celebrations of Life." These events are usually planned anytime from thirty to sixty days after the death. Celebrations are held in private homes, in churches or synagogues, at favorite restaurants or clubs, and in a variety of outdoor venues that had special meaning to the deceased. They often include favorite music, balloons, much humor and are like big parties. Since people in the gay community come from diverse families of origin and carry a package of mixed beliefs, having new, unique to them, rituals is especially meaningful to the survivors. These rituals are created in a loving, safe, accepting environment that honors and respects the gay orientation.

Benjamin was *I Love Lucy*'s biggest fan. He had a collection of memorabilia that filled rooms of his home. Meeting Lucy was one of the highlights of his life. When he died, his friends decided that the best celebration of his life would be to share his love for Lucy with all who attended his service even if it seemed "campy." The theme song from the show greeted people as they walked into the hall. They were surprised by this seemingly irreverent action but then they started chuckling. They remembered Benjamin's love and how much fun he had collecting all the pictures and books that were displayed here. There was even a monitor with a constant showing of Benjamin's video tape collection of the shows. People were laughing and truly celebrating the life of a friend who had given them so much joy. Many of them said, "Benjamin would have loved this. It was all so much a part of who he was."

Helpers who are familiar with, sensitive to, and understanding about, diverse cultural and ethnic issues can be found in many cities. Anyone who is willing to be part of a support system for mourners, but less knowledgeable about differences, needs to find appropriate resources to help survivors reconnect to previous traditions or to establish new rituals and sources of spiritual support if they so desire. When individual cultural, religious, spiritual beliefs, and expectations are known and accepted by both the survivors and the helpers, mourning becomes a more positive and meaningful experience.

REFERENCES

1. S. Jue, AIDS and Cross-Cultural Counseling, *FOCUS: A Guide to AIDS Research and Counseling,* 3:10, p. 3, September, AIDS Health Project, University of California San Francisco, 1988.
2. Fairfax County, Virginia, *Crisis Intervention for Child Fatalities: A Guide for Child Service Providers,* Department of Human Development, 1994.

CHAPTER 12

For Mental Health Professionals

Grief counseling or grief therapy

It is often difficult to distinguish between grief counseling and grief therapy [1]. Many grief counselors feel inadequately trained for the more complex problems one might find when dealing with a mourner who is overly emotional, needy, or very distressed. Therapists might find themselves describing the grief reactions as diagnosable mental disorders, in order to have an insurance company pay for treatment. Doing so implies that intense grief is a "condition" as opposed to the reality that it is a normal response.

It is always wise, no matter whether one calls oneself a counselor or a therapist, to be honest about one's own abilities, limitations, and interests. Specific tasks are therefore recommended for the mental health professional offering support to those persons who are mourning someone who died of AIDS-related illness. These tasks are necessary for anyone dealing with the multiple losses of this disease. The first task is to work toward increasing self-awareness in regard to death issues. As a therapist, it would be wise to be sensitive to the existential issues of confronting death. Many survivors of multiple loss become preoccupied with their own mortality, creating a sense of dread, existential anxiety, and other feelings associated with personal death awareness. The task here is to provide an environment for the person to talk about these feelings and to acknowledge that there may be no answers to the client's difficult and challenging philosophical questions. It is a time to help the survivor understand that dying is something that we all must do to complete our life cycle. How we accept or assist other in accepting this concept is the challenge.

A clinician working in the area of AIDS-related multiple losses will experience many deaths. Some of these deaths are personal losses and others are the losses experienced by survivors who come for help. Counselors working in AIDS service organizations will experience a barrage of multiple and ongoing deaths that is frequently the cause of staff turnover. While these organizations offer many support groups for their clients, there are not many groups for the professionals who staff the agencies. This means that clinicians must find a way to deal with their work-related grief and any unfinished grief related to their personal lives. The emotional reactions of a professional to the devastation caused by AIDS are no less important than those of the clients. Counselors who do not understand their own issues around death and dying will it find difficult to be fully available to those they hope to help.

Mental health professionals who are HIV-positive have additional issues to deal with that might include:

Concerns about their continuing ability to work,

Confronting their own death,

Complicated grieving around their own personal losses and those of the clients,

Whether or not to share their serostatus with colleagues and/or clients.

These are difficult issues to confront and point up the need for the professional to be open to seeking counseling and support for him or herself while helping the mourners.

The second task involves understanding one's attitude toward AIDS. Those who died of this disease were mostly members of populations that are stigmatized and discriminated against in most societies in the United States. The clinicians' attitude has to be examined and brought into awareness. What are his or her attitudes toward people of different cultures, races and ethnic groups; substance abusers; and those practicing behaviors considered to be out of the norm? Counselors need to be comfortable with and non judgmental about a variety of sexual orientations and practices, and not place value judgments on how HIV infection occurred. The work at hand with a grieving survivor is to do grief work, not to change the mourner or challenge his or her way of life.

The next task includes increasing one's knowledge in the following areas:

- Feelings and stages of grief,
- HIV and AIDS,
- Variety of religious and cultural belief and practices around death and mourning,
- Power and consequences of secrets and secret-keeping.

Skilled professionals realize that the survivor may tell and retell the story or stories of the losses and recognize that this need is not pathological. Multiple loss is quite overwhelming and clients often need to express themselves by telling the same story over and over again. Doing so provides opportunities to begin to integrate the deceased into the life of the griever.

Most therapists know how important it is to offer a safe environment for the mourners. Holding survivor support groups in a neutral location may be helpful. Caregivers can find it difficult to come back to a place that has memories of the pain, suffering, dependency issues and other illness-related activities. Recognizing the need for support may not be enough to bring them to the group if it is held in an environment that they are trying to avoid.

Growing self-awareness and understanding of one's attitudes is an ongoing task especially for mental health professionals. This work will co-exist with the following tasks that relate to the therapeutic work with the mourner:

- Evaluate and define the nature of the mourner's relationship with the deceased, including the meaning and value to the survivor of time spent with that person. In order to be effective, this must be done in a non- judgmental, open, and safe fashion. Counselors must constantly be aware of the complexity of nontraditional relationships, and the inescapable role played by homophobia and social stigmatization. The efforts of gay survivors to work through the grief process are made worse by the homophobia that pervades most societies. Awareness of any homophobic attitude is important for a counselor.

- If the survivor seeking support is a gay man, the counselor may uncover feelings of internalized homophobia in this mourner. These feelings often are focused on other gay men whom he sees as possibly having AIDS. This attitude can cause the mourner to isolate himself and withdraw from previous support systems. Internalized homophobia may be manifested by the mourner in self-hatred or shame in being gay and seeing AIDS as punishment. Family members and friends may be homophobic blaming the survivor for the death of their family member or friend. These misled homophobic beliefs can lead to depression and isolation. Bringing these beliefs into awareness can facilitate discussion and lead to prevention of psychological problems.

- Exploring and evaluating previous losses, especially in childhood, is important. This history is useful in identifying unfinished grief work and laying the groundwork for a more systematic assessment of coping skills, suicide risk, and self-destructive tendencies. A survivor's way of coping with previous crises need to be explored. During the exploration the helper will find out what worked for the survivors and what didn't work when they faced stressful situations. Explore the personal strengths they bring to this particular situation or any other situations related to other death experiences. A personality profile to assess behavior patterns is helpful. Accurate assessment of coping skills is particularly important, given that the survivor's coping ability is mediated by his or her own health status, by the number and chronology of previously experienced deaths, and by the nature of the relationship to the deceased.

Allen, a member of the grief support group, had been in a long-term monogamous relationship. During routine testing he was found to have a depressed immune system. He heard the report and immediately considered suicide. He had engaged in one episode of unprotected sex with someone after an argument with his partner. He regretted this instance of promiscuity and he continued to feel guilty thinking he gave HIV to his now deceased lover. He was beset by fears for his own health and said he would kill himself before he suffered the same way his lover had suffered before he died. As he expressed these fears other group members began to share similar thoughts and feelings.

Continual reality testing is necessary to alleviate the disorientation experienced with this syndrome of multiple loss. Reality testing means that we pointed out to Allen that he recently had the flu and that he was deeply grieving the death of his lover. Either of which could have an effect on the immune system and he was urged to see his doctor for confirmation. In Allen's case, this discussion demonstrated that learning facts about the immune system and sharing his experiences in group offered social support that is a protective variable against illness. He was able to put his experience in perspective, start to take care of himself, and let go of his thoughts of suicide.

One major challenge for the therapist is to clearly differentiate actual clinical depression from other AIDS-related symptoms and from normal grief. There is a great deal of overlay among symptom patterns because of grief feelings and/or central nervous system involvement in the case of those with AIDS. Examples of overlapping symptoms include fatigue, insomnia, weight loss, anorexia and other somatic complaints.

The following chart (page 112) shows the possible distinctions between depression of grief and clinical depression [2].

It is necessary to evaluate factors such as general life dissatisfaction, crying spells, decision-making difficulties, suicidal ideation, and loss of interest in social activities and friends. It is helpful to be aware of drug and medication usage especially with PLWA, as this often has an effect on one's mental status. Some PLWA are living with mild-to-serious problems of dementia and the counselor will want to be aware of this possibility. The importance of a multidisciplinary support team for the infected mourner cannot be stressed enough. Dialogues between the members of the team help them define responsibilities, share concerns, discuss treatments, and understand the best interests of the patient.

Normal Grief	Clinical Depression
Responds to comfort and support	Does not accept support
Often openly angry	Irritable and may complain, but does not directly express anger
Relates depressed feelings to loss experienced	Does not relate experiences to a particular life event
Can still experience moments of enjoyment in life	Exhibits an all pervading sense of doom
Exhibits feelings of sadness and emptiness	Projects a sense of hopelessness and chronic emptiness
May have transient physical complaints	Has chronic physical complaints
Expresses guilt over some specific aspect of the loss	Has generalized feelings of guilt
Has temporary impact on self-esteem	Loss of self-esteem is of greater duration

Many mourners of multiple losses describe themselves as experiencing numbness or lack of feeling that becomes worse with each death. It is helpful for therapists to reframe this numbness as "compassionate detachment," an acquired ability that allows survivors to remain involved without experiencing bereavement overload or burnout. Reassuring mourners that they are still caring, sensitive people allows them to grieve without believing that they are failures.

A clinician may find some mourners experiencing emotional problems as a result of changes around HIV treatment. Eugene Wells discusses the emotional backlash for those who had resigned themselves to AIDS as a terminal illness [3]. There is the realization that this mindset may no longer work. Feelings of regret from past choices may become a central theme of counseling. A sense of wasted or lost time may emerge as people consider choices such a quitting school, not saving money, selling life insurance policies, running up debts, or engaging in health-compromising behaviors.

Place these concerns in context and remind the mourner that people often make similar choices when faced with expected death. Now is the time to explore AIDS-related losses and the feelings they are experiencing as a result of surviving when so many others have died. The survivor guilt that may be experienced can now be understood. There may be regrets for the mourner, but he can be encouraged to find a focus for the future with goals that are possible to achieve.

Counselors who have accomplished the above tasks and are comfortable with the intense emotions of grief will find this work rewarding. By increasing self-awareness and by understanding AIDS-grief they will be able to guide the survivor by:

- Asking the grieving person explicitly: "What would be most helpful for you at this time?" By responding to expressed needs, the therapeutic relationship evolves, trust builds, and there is shared decision making.
- Talking about the multiple losses which then helps the mourner accept the reality,
- Teaching the survivors about typical grief reactions,
- Understanding that mourners' responses are individual and that there is no right or wrong way to grieve,
- Giving the mourner hope—someday the pain will decrease and life will have meaning again,
- Helping survivors find new meaning in life without those who died, and,
- Providing them with community resources and information to be accessed as needed.

A mental health professional fulfills many roles as the needs of survivors change throughout the grief process. The roles range from being a parent, advocate, fighter, technician, or teacher in response to the mourner sometimes being a child, victim, consumer, or student.

A competent professional will be aware of opportunities to self-disclose while still maintaining boundaries. Knowing when to self-disclose is especially important in the case of a professional who is grieving, who is HIV-positive and/or is a member of an affected community. This is a sensitive issue as premature self-disclosure can be threatening to the survivor and can make him feel as if he doesn't count and that the helper is more important. Whereas, sharing one's similarities and coping skills related to the problem, at an appropriate moment, can offer role modeling behavior for the person who is grieving.

The grief surrounding HIV/AIDS is unique, made so by societal stigmatization of those infected and by the multiple losses that occur. Therapy can offer options, suggestions, resources and coping skills that lead to resolution of grief. Clinicians knowledgeable about grief and loss can ease the pain and assist in enhancing the quality of life for those who come to them for support during this horrendous pandemic as well as for themselves. Along with treating survivors, clinicians are encouraged to understand and explore their own unfinished grief work. This exploration will enable them to deal with their emotional reactions to this devastation. Doing the work of grief resolution can lead to an understanding of parts of one's life that are unresolved and, possibly interfering with client work and personal fulfillment.

The experiences gained by mental health professionals who deal with this disease can be used to influence public policy and to support legislation to provide funding for those affected and for those infected. The opportunities for caring and support are practically limitless. As future generations look back on HIV/AIDS, let us hope they see that those in the helping professions rose to the challenge.

REFERENCES

1. J. W. Worden, *Grief Counseling Therapy*, Springer, New York, 1991.
2. A. D. Wolfelt, *Death and Grief: A Guide for Clergy*, Accelerated Development, Inc., Muncie, Indiana (permission to use granted by author), 1988.
3. E. Wells, New Prognosis for HIV: A Mental Health Perspective, in *HIV Frontline, 26*, p. 4, World Health CME, New York, January/February 1996.

CHAPTER 13

What to Look For in a Clinician

When dealing with AIDS-related grief

Virtually every aspect of a person's life is changed upon the death of a significant other. As the reality of the loss "hits home," the mourner becomes painfully aware of the broader implications for his or her life. There are adjustments to make, transitions to experience, and consequences for the changes in their lives. The usual support systems that help one deal with life crises may not be adequate for these complicated issues. The grieving person recognizes the need to talk to someone who can offer a safe environment to sort, understand, and examine these feelings and concerns. Mourners are encouraged to talk about their experiences and to find peer or professional support during this painful time. The services of mental health professionals, familiar with grief work, are valuable. Their guidance can assure that the grievers realize that their experiences are normal.

Does it matter if the helper is gay or straight? Male or female? Same or different race? These are valid questions for someone to ask when seeking support. Many people will be uncomfortable interviewing a counselor but the interview process enables the mourner to choose a counselor with whom he or she feels rapport. This is a difficult task when one is hurting, but feeling cared for and understood insures the success of the experience.

When seeking a mental health professional to help with grief work, survivors will want to look for someone who is:

- Aware that the job at hand is to do grief work, not to change the way of life of the client;
- Ethical, non-judgmental, flexible, accepting, appropriately self-disclosing, willing to learn, and who has a sense of humor;
- Aware of his or her attitudes, thoughts, and responses to a variety of sexual orientations and behaviors;
- Understanding and aware of key issues related to HIV/AIDS, including local community resources and responses. Able to create supportive networks for PLWA and for helpers in communities that may be isolated or unfriendly;
- Familiar with the specific skills needed for grief counseling, including the willingness to help the mourner learn to live with and without the deceased;
- Able to just listen, realizing that there will not always be an answer to certain questions. Willing to answer questions openly and honestly;
- Clear about the limits of his or her availability and involvement with HIV/AIDS to prevent burnout and to model healthy caregiving;
- Able to differentiate between the symptoms of depression and similar symptoms of AIDS;
- Aware of drug and medication use and interactions;
- Trained to assess coping skills, suicide risk, destructive behaviors, sexual practices, alcohol and drug use, stress reduction techniques, and all support systems;
- Willing to take a history identifying previous losses that might need ongoing grief work;
- Aware of the need to do continual reality testing, since coping with multiple loss is often disorienting;
- Aware that the survivor may also be grieving the loss of the role of caregiver, an often overlooked aftereffect of death;
- Able to define the nature of the relationship of client to the deceased, including the meaning to the survivor of the time they spent together;
- Understanding of the survivor's need to tell and retell his or her story as part of the grief recovery process;

- Aware that keeping secrets may have been part of the relationship history and that those secrets now need to be told;
- Supportive of a healthy lifestyle for the client as well as for him/herself, including but not limited to proper eating, exercise, and relaxation;
- Aware that grieving for multiple losses is not considered pathological;
- Respectful of the client's cultural and spiritual beliefs or willing to explore possibilities if none currently exist or there is confusion about one's belief system;
- Thoughtfully providing a safe environment for the exploration of feelings;
- Lastly, a mental health professional will be willing to repeat information patiently, as mourners can experience stress, denial, and/or cognitive impairment which prevents them from assimilating information.

There is an ongoing need to find ways to cope with the many deaths and losses related to HIV/AIDS. Survivors who are grieving these multipe losses often try to find a way to ascribe meaning to their lives. These thoughts and feelings can be explored in a supportive environment. A mourner will learn to recognize that feeling the pain of the losses is not to be feared. In reality, it is the first step toward resolution of the grief. Working hard to resolve the grief does not mean learning to let go of the loved ones who have died. It does mean maintaining a relationship to the deceased by learning to make the deceased and the loving memories a part of one's ongoing life.

CHAPTER 14

Coping and Survival Skills

Healing ways and specific skills for coping with grief

... how do you survive grief and loss? I'd say isolate what you love, and pursue that with everything you're worth.
Bill T. Jones, dancer [1]

Most mourners do not realize that they have a choice in how they heal from their grief. Grieving can continue as long as necessary, but, at the same time, the survivor can move into a healthy pattern of living. Helpers try to encourage and support the mourner in this process. Those who assist grievers as they move through their grief, can become frustrated if they experience disinterest and resistance from the griever. But people have different ways of moving through grief. Those who are mourning can learn to give themselves permission to feel better by exploring some or all of the coping skills discussed in this chapter.

There are ways to survive the painful process of grief. Some say it is helpful to become a workaholic. Others think that the solution is to keep busy with a hobby, volunteer activities, or travel. Still others tell friends who are grieving to join a support group. Although reasonable, these suggestions are sometimes hard to follow. Mourners may feel concern that by following the suggestions and beginning to feel better, they may lose their link to the one who died. If the intense feelings of connection diminish, does that mean that the deceased is moving farther away? Will even memories of loved ones be lost? When people realize there are ways to keep the deceased with them for as long as they want, their fears of feeling better are reduced. They become aware that those who have died will always play an important part in one's life; that they are not lost but are just present in a different way.

Grieving styles are very different and there is no "right way" to grieve. Mourners often find that those around them have definite ideas of how one "should" experience grief and express feelings. One man in our support group was unable to throw away his deceased partner's toothbrush. He wasn't ready to discard it. Another group member insisted that the toothbrush had to go. He himself had gotten rid of his partner's belongings because the sight of them made him cry. Our group worked on supporting the concept that each person has to be comfortable with his or her own way of grieving.

Perhaps the following questions asked by the mourners in our group sound familiar. "Is there a way to bring meaning to the loss that will help me to survive?" "How can I learn to cope with the absence of my loved one?" "How can I motivate myself to begin the healing process?" "How can I walk through the grief, putting the pain behind me, and still stay close and connected to the deceased?"

Group members found it helpful to answer these questions by exploring the following activities or coping strategies that can be used by anyone who is mourning.

Identify Stresses in the Mourners' Life

Those who *feel* under excess stress, *are* under excess stress. People may say, "You have no reason to be stressed," but if you feel that way, it is important to trust those feelings. After identifying stresses, one can then choose to make changes that will alter the level of stress. Some hidden stresses to uncover might include unrealistic goals, such as the need to be perfect or the need to always be on time. Keeping one's sexual orientation hidden can be a source of great stress and there may be relief if one chooses to "come out of the closet." Pressures of home and job cause many to feel stressed. Some mourners find solace and relief in the monotony of everyday tasks. but others may feel overwhelmed and stressed by their responsibilities. As mourners are helped to reevaluate their obligations, they find more energy to be relaxed and productive.

Mourners can make a list of their daily and weekly activities and to identify how much time is spent in pursuit. Looking at their list, they can identify which activities are done out of obligation (because they have always been done a certain way.) They will be able to see which activities are engaged in because saying "no" was not possible even though there is no desire to participate. Evaluate which tasks offer solace and relief and which cause additional stress. Once most obligations are identified, one can begin to choose those to eliminate. David Seabury teaches that there is a great art to selfishness. He advises that those who are able to take care of themselves can be more productive, less stressed and of greater value to others. Encourage the survivor to examine the completed list of activities in order to set priorities and goals keeping "selfishness" in mind [2]. Have him or her identify the items that are non-negotiable like going to work or taking prescribed medicine, and put these at the top of the list. He or she can be helped to reevaluate each of the other items to decide if or where they belong on the list.

Exploring possible ways to share obligations and activities with friends or neighbors is one way to make them easier and less stressful. If driving is stressful, perhaps a carpool can be arranged. Responsibility for chores may be delegated, such as dividing the planning and cooking of meals. Planning a reward to be enjoyed after the chore is completed gives all those involved something to look forward to, reducing the stress related to the task.

Even one's attitude toward doing chores can be changed by looking for different ways to accomplish them. When this topic came up in the support group, Edward shared that he hated the ironing that always accumulated after the weekly laundry. He was complaining to a neighbor who said that she actually enjoyed ironing but hated to vacuum. Since Edward didn't mind that chore, they traded. He got freshly ironed clothes and she ended up with a clean house.

Focus on Soothing Activities

Start by making a list of activities that feel soothing to you. Perhaps taking walks, relaxing in a Jacuzzi or enjoying fine dining. Once the list is completed, you can pull out the activities that are currently manageable. Choose one each week to incorporate into your daily routine.

Resting one's mind as well as one's body is important in order to relieve stresses. Quiet time gives a much-needed mental vacation. The following exercise in relaxation and imaging can be done in a time span of twenty minutes or less. Once imagined, the images will then be available to recall as needed.

Start by sitting in a comfortable position. Close your eyes. Take several slow, deep breaths. As you exhale, allow the stress in your body to float away with each breath. Let your mind become free with no thoughts or ideas. Open your mind to let in an image of a place where you feel peaceful. It might be a familiar locale or one you've never been to. Let yourself be surprised. Take time to use each of your senses to experience this peaceful space. Look around you and see what is there. Smell the air and savor the fragrance. Touch and feel the things in the environment. Listen to sounds that might fill the air. Savor the feelings of peace and calm.

Once this vision has been seen, calmness can be found in the midst of whatever is happening in life. Close your eyes for a few moments and revisit your peaceful place. Take several deep breaths again. Recreate the calm feeling.

Take Vacations from Death

When caregivers allow themselves to take occasional vacations from death, they temporarily avoid the ongoing reminders that are so difficult to bear. For those who live in a community where people are constantly dying of AIDS, dealing with the loss of loved ones reflects the reality that there is no way to avoid this disease. The world is infected and we all need to be aware of how it affects each of us. AIDS death is not going away soon but one does return from a time-out feeling somewhat refreshed and able to face ongoing activities and responsibilities.

Help the survivor use his or her list of soothing activities as a base for choosing a place to go away from one's daily routines. Give him or her permission to take a vacation to this chosen location, knowing that as he or she feels comforted, there will also be regeneration of energy. Upon the return the mourner will have increased energy both for self and for those who need support.

Short trips out of town or even a night or two in a different location in the city in which he lives will offer this respite. If a survivor is HIV-positive and/or has AIDS or other diseases involving complicated medical regimens, have him obtain his medical provider's approval to alter or modify his prescribed program. This will provide a change of pace and offer a different perspective on the obligations of one's life.

When a survivor/caregiver does take time off, engaging in engrossing activities will refresh and challenge. It is hard to maintain a negative stress level when concentrating on not falling off a bicycle or on swimming a few laps.

Explore the Arts

As one explores death, one can also explore the meaning of life by participating in creative arts programs. One can participate as an observer by attending events in the city in which one lives. Mourners can also participate by exploring their own creativity. Playing an instrument, dancing, writing creatively or joining a choral group are all healing ways to express oneself and one's feelings. As a survivor gets in touch with the hopefulness and beauty of life through music, art or drama, dull feelings will lessen.

Encourage the mourner to write letters to the loved one who died. This will create an opportunity to share previously unsaid thoughts and feelings. It is also a way for the survivor to get in touch with unfinished business that will affect the resolution of grief. Carlene couldn't let go of her anger after her business partner succumbed to one of the AIDS-related opportunistic infections. They had worked extremely hard for several years building their consulting business. Each of them brought a different perspective to the clients they served and they were finally successful. "How could he do this to me?" she ranted. "What am I going to do now?" She then got angry at herself for even saying these words so selfishly. "I know he didn't want to get sick and die. But I just can't forgive him."

I suggested that she sit down and write Mike a letter. This uncensored letter would include everything she wanted to say to him. At first she thought it was a silly idea to write a letter to a dead man but she was getting desperate for relief from the anger and she finally started writing. She told him how angry she was, she told him how much she missed him and then she found herself telling him all about the business. "What a surprise!" She said. "I can't believe I'm writing all this. It feels like I am close to him again. I know he is dead but it still feels like he is with me and can help guide me. I even know what he would say to the president of that small company we just took on. After all, we did build this business together."

Volunteer to Help Those Less Fortunate

We all have skills and talents at various levels that we can share with others. Perhaps someone who likes to bake or garden can volunteer to bring "goodies" to the local food bank or hospice. People are often surprised to find that giving to others will restore one's own lost energy.

Use Anger to Empower Not Depress

Anger is one of the most prevalent emotions related to multiple loss and holding it in can cause physical pain. Anger can be focused, harnessed and its emotional energy used to move one forward in a positive way. If one gives oneself permission to acknowledge the anger and have it validated, it can be directed into healthy modes such as exercising, dancing, drawing or painting, writing, public speaking, or political action. Each of these are ways to express the anger. Redirecting the anger will provide increased energy to explore other emotions that may be deterrents to living life to its fullest.

Anger can also be channeled into action to make changes and to rectify issues so others won't have to die the same way as the deceased. Gatherings and marches are frequently organized around a cause that often stems from mistreatment and mis-understanding. Survivors can become politically active and involved to continue the passions and interests of their loved ones.

Pay Attention to Self-Care, Grooming, Exercise, Relaxation, and Nutrition

In the mid-to-late 1980s, George Solomon and his colleagues in San Francisco studied long-term survivors who were living with AIDS and published a list of their attributes [3]. Because grief has an impact on the status of a survivor's health, mastering some or all of these qualities can also give *any* mourner more control over his life thereby increasing longevity and decreasing illness. The list developed by Dr. Solomon and his team included some of the following traits and common denominators that continue to be relavent today:

- Perceiving health care as a collaboration between patient and doctor,
- Becoming educated about one's personal health issues in order to participate in treatment decisions,
- Having a sense of meaningfulness and purpose in life and finding a new meaning as a result of the disease,
- Accepting diagnosis but not seeing it as a "death sentence,"
- Being assertive and learning to say "no" in order to withdraw from taxing involvements and to nurture oneself,
- Communicating openly about the illness and one's concerns,
- Being sensitive to one's body and to physical and psychological needs.

Along with exploring the attributes of being a long-term survivor, one has to become aware of activities and behaviors that may, in fact, be self-defeating or self-destructive. There is a common tendency to make impulsive changes during grief to "run away" from the pain. Some who are grieving want to sell the home they shared with the deceased. This often impulsive act can cause them to lose a great deal of money in the sale. Others quit jobs and move out of the city where memories are too painful for them to remain. Because the pain is so intense, survivors sometime become suicidal with an unconscious desire to escape the pain and join the loved one who died. But one cannot run away from grief. It will "follow" mourners until it is acknowledged. So it is important to encourage mourners to seek professional help to explore issues that may be self-defeating. After one has acquired an awareness of these behaviors, healthier, less impulsive changes can be made.

Survivors may turn to drugs, alcohol or "comfort" foods to try to numb the pain of grief. This is not an uncommon response. However, these behaviors, when carried to excess, take away physical, emotional, and psychosocial well-being. "Comfort" foods are often foods filled with fats and sugars that may produce instant highs but are quickly followed by depressive lows. The comfort is short lived. The guilt and increased negative self-image are not.

As part of taking good care of oneself, the survivor can try to develop a new definition for "comfort" food. Choose a favorite fruit or vegetable and transform it into a "feeling good" food. Imagine it providing vitamins and minerals to heal the grief and make one stronger. Find out about the positive effects of using natural vitamin and mineral supplements. Give strokes when eating healthy foods by reminding oneself that doing so is taking care. Occasionally satisfying the urge for snack foods can be OK without judging and punishing oneself.

The value of drinking water is often forgotten. Remember to drink water frequently. Imagine the cool, refreshing, cleansing liquid wash away excess amounts of pain and disease. As the toxins are washed away, imagine the free space inside filling with peace and quiet. As changes are made, listen to what the body has to say. Trust what is heard.

Understand That You Always Have Choices

Almost everything one does involves making a choice. Choices are made using the best alternatives one has in any situation with current knowledge and resources. Yet, we can get stuck in believing we had no choices when none of the alternatives seem to give us what we want. Try listing the options available in each situation and it will be obvious that there are always choices. The secret is in the acceptance of one choice knowing it is the best one available. Armed with this knowledge one can let go of what was not chosen without being regretful later. Learning to accept choices helps one take control by identifying those areas in which one can still be in charge. For example, saying "no" to unpleasant situations is an important way of taking care of oneself.

Use Support Systems as a Forum for Sharing Information and for Discussion of Feelings and Stresses

Survivors may feel abandoned by the person who died. One will find becoming actively involved with social and/or therapeutic support systems and networks affords opportunities to discuss feelings and problems. Mourners will soon find that they are not alone. Reaching out and connecting with others will help one explore and reduce uncomfortable and scary feelings.

Paul felt very abandoned and isolated after his partner died. He had tears in his eyes the first time he was asked to join in a group hug. He confessed to having had fears of becoming contaminated by touching his deceased lover. Because of these fears, he now felt guilty and sad that he had withheld much needed physical affection. Sharing this information allowed other group members to admit to almost no physical contact with another person since their partners had become ill. They realized how much they missed the touching. After this they were able to hug each other in the group. The displays of physical affection then extended outside the group where they were able to reconnect to friends and family members.

Avoid the temptation to totally withdraw. Finding a balance between solitude and socializing can help one feel less alone. As mourners identify people around them who have been, and will continue to be, supportive and available, they can arrange involvement with those supporters. Survivors will become aware of feeling safe and comfortable when in the presence of caring people and will continue to be surrounded by them during the time of healing.

Support groups, usually led by professionals, can help with exploring the meaning of one's losses. These groups will also help the mourner understand feelings so he or she will not feel "crazy." The support group leader will also show how to incorporate loss experiences into life. The connections made in a group around a shared issue will give the survivor strength for his or her life outside the group. Those who make up a support system will help counter the conspiracy of silence that often occurs during grief because mourners often believe that no one could possibly understand how they feel. Sharing in the group setting increases the comfort level of the mourner allowing him or her to be able to talk more openly and freely about the person who died.

Nurture Hope

Hope means different things to different people at different times. The object of hope can also change. At some point we may wish for the recovery of our loved one. As his health worsens, we hope for less suffering. Then we hope for release and peace. We still maintain hope but what we hope for has changed. Preserving even a tiny bit of hope is essential for surviving the pressures of this AIDS-related caregiving situation. Without hope one is not able to move forward in life. Helpers must learn to balance accurate empathy for the hopelessness felt by those they are supporting with encouragement and belief that the mourner will be able to overcome the situation.

One of the men in my support group shared the following thoughts: "The experience associated with multiple deaths, though mostly negative, does have a hopeful side. Because the numbers are outside the normal, I, in my effort to try to "figure it out," have been forced to do a great deal of "inside of me" investigation to become more enlightened." As Reece explored his belief systems and values, he realized that he was a very talented productive person who had a lot to offer his friends and co-workers. He became more hopeful of surviving the despair and pain of his grief by continuing his work, making new friends, and taking care of himself.

In response to Reece's self-acceptance, Charlie, another group member, said, "That may work for you but, boy, I read all this stuff about how peaceful death is and how spiritual and how wonderful it is to be with people at the moment of death but I want to tell you that it isn't all it's cut out to be. I was with Joe when he died and he was still depressed and angry and really scared. I couldn't do anything for him. There was no hope of him finding spiritual peace. How am I going to live with that helpless feeling?" There are no easy, reassuring answers to questions like Charlie's. Helpers can offer the following:

- try to help the survivors focus on what they did do for the deceased;
- remind them that people's personality and mood swings are deeply ingrained and not easily resolved even when death is approaching;
- help the mourners get in touch with their own spiritual beliefs, and discuss the possibility that the feelings held onto so tightly in life may not go with one in death.

Perhaps there is comfort in that thought, and after all, the helper's role is to foster hope in whatever way will support the one who is in need.

Andrea told me, "It's about having support and resources so when you feel scared with things in life you can talk to someone. You can look with a positive attitude at the things that scare you and have hope instead of despair." Survivors can try to think of, and make a list of all the things to hope for to create positiveness out of pain. One possibility could be hoping that there will just be enough energy to continue with life. Wanting what one hopes for can motivate one to find ways to accomplish it.

Connect or Reconnect with a Religious/Spiritual Base

Homosexuality and AIDS create conflicts between the teachings of some religions and the love and compassion some family members feel toward PLWA. The conflict raises questions of a spiritual or religious nature because AIDS is often seen as a punishment from God. Because people are influenced by religious teachings that condemn gays, they often feel guilty for not caring enough or for believing they caused the PLWA to be gay. If the mourner is estranged from his religion, he may feel as if he betrayed early teachings of his family. Exploring spiritual options that will benefit one at this time in life can ease the stress of trying to cope with ongoing loss. Even if organized religion is unappealing, comfort can be found in exploring spirituality. When the differences between religion and spirituality are explored, expressed, and shared, the social support that comes from being part of a religious or spiritual gathering is enriching.

Many religious leaders now ask forgiveness for their religious institutions' previous negative judgments about homosexuality. They suggest that it is possible to forgive the perceived wrongs, without forgetting, in order to find the value in reconnecting to one's tradition. Doing so allows one to share the positives spirituality can bring. A church, synagogue, or religious and/or spiritual community to become involved in can offer support. Especially if it is open to dealing with AIDS and multiple loss issues. Changes in many denominations make them more welcoming. Perhaps it is time to explore an environment or discipline that will be new and different from earlier experiences. Even if one is not affiliated with a particular denomination, it is still possible to attend and participate in services.

Meditation can be part of the experience of spirituality. It is a way to reflect on or contemplate in a spiritual way that which is happening in one's life. Pondering, weighing, thinking through, or deliberating in this manner helps one put events in perspective and gain control of often overwhelming situations. Meditation can be explored as another tool to be used in the pursuit of continuing physical and mental health during resolution of grief.

Dream encounters or hallucinations (false or distorted perception of objects, persons, or events that feel very real), with those who have died are both normal and very powerful. They can be visual, thinking we see the deceased person; auditory, believing we hear their voice; or olfactory, meaning that we smell a fragrance associated with the person who died. These hallucinations often allow us to complete unfinished or unresolved business. During one of the group sessions, Jeffrey told us about the following experience: "Two days ago I walked into my kitchen to make dinner. There was a very strong, familiar smell in the room. All of a sudden I realized that it was the aftershave that Teddy always wore. I moved into this apartment a year after he died and he was obviously never here. I got really freaked out and started searching the rooms for him. I finally remembered what you said about hallucinations and realized that the smell was in my mind. I wanted him to be there. I finally calmed down and tried to talk to him, or his ghost or whatever. It felt real nice to reconnect with him but I sure don't know why it was through that unusual aftershave."

After hearing Jeffrey's story others began to share similar experiences. One man recalled seeing his Bible open to a passage that had relevance for him and his deceased lover. He never shared that experience because he thought anyone he told it to would think that he was losing his mind. Brad talked about walking down the street and catching a glimpse of a man by a car. He was sure that it was his dead lover. He started to walk over to the man and then realized what he was doing. He has caught himself several other times also. Sharing his experience in the group made him feel more normal about these events and he began looking forward to opportunities to "see" his friend.

Annette told us her dream: "Eddie died a few months before his thirtieth birthday and we had been planning a big celebration. He really wanted to have that party and I was so upset that we never had a chance to do what we planned. The night of his birthday I dreamt that I was in a large hall with all of our friends. There was a grand staircase coming down from an entry area. All of a sudden there was a great flash of light and Eddie was standing at the top of the stairs looking gorgeous and healthy. He came down the stairs with a big smile and we saw that he was carrying a birthday cake decorated with tulips, the flowers he loved the most. I woke up feeling so happy, like we did have a celebration after all. Maybe his whole life with me was one big celebration. It was a wonderful dream." When we learn to welcome those who died as they walk through our life and dreams we will not be frightened by the visions.

Develop and Participate in Rituals

Grief has a rightful place in life, and one of the ways to try to make sense of death is to engage in symbolic rituals and ceremonies, both personal and shared. In so doing, we honor ourselves and memorialize those who have died. A specific behavior or activity becomes a symbolic expression of feelings and thoughts related to a death. Rituals become tools for examining grief in a positive, life-affirming way. Using rituals enables survivors to accept the reality of the loss and helps them keep the deceased in their life. One ritual involves replacing the physical presence of the deceased with a tangible object that will enrich the lives of the survivors. Planting a tree in memory of the deceased is one often observed ritual.

George and Jose were very active, much loved volunteers at one of the AIDS food banks in Los Angeles. They both died of AIDS-related illnesses within a week of each other and the loss felt by the staff was overwhelming. Everyone chipped in money and bought a ficus tree with intertwined branches. The tree was placed in the lobby of the building where everyone passed by as they came to work. They said "hello" to the two men each day, watered and cared for "them" regularly and constantly felt the living presence of these men in the growing tree. They knew that George and Jose would love this tribute. With the planting of the tree, not only was there something tangible, but the presence of the tree gave the mourners permission to express feelings, find an acceptable outlet for grief, and have a symbol to focus upon. The rituals channeled the grief into a manageable and less overwhelming experience with a clear purpose.

Many survivors I have worked with agonize over how to remember all those who have died. During one session of a support group I was leading, when we dealt with this topic, the group members decided they would select an object to represent LOSS. They each decided to light a big round candle at a certain time of day when a deceased loved one came to mind. Lighting the candle allowed then to focus on death and loss for a few moments of designated time. This way death did not have to be an overwhelming constant in their lives.

Additionally, knowing they had this ritual, enabled them to "tell" their loved ones that a special time had been set aside for reflection. This was a way to reduce the feelings of guilt experienced when they realized that their thoughts were frequently on other than the deceased. This ritual helped focus the grief, allowed time for expression of feelings and helped the mourners move toward resolution. Some of the men in the group talked of lighting candles when they wanted to be in touch with those living with HIV. They wanted to maintain a spiritual connection with the living, not just with the dead. Lighting a candle became a meaningful way to affirm life as well as to remember those who had died.

In anticipation of the Olympic events in Atlanta, Georgia in 1996, the women quilters of this state made quilts for the participating countries' representatives. A display of these quilts was shown in Macon. One of the quilters was acting as a docent on the day we arrived at the museum. I asked her if she was familiar with the AIDS Memorial Quilt. She replied, "The curator of this museum died of AIDS-related illnesses and I made a quilt panel for him. I took it to my local quilting society meeting to share. A small, but vocal, group of women present protested this public display of something they found shameful. Boy, was I upset. They all loved him and yet acted this way. I couldn't believe it!"

I asked her what she did about their response and she said, "I went to the National Association of Quilters and asked them what their policy was. They told me to continue displaying my AIDS quilt. They were not only in favor of the quilt, they emphasized the educational benefit. I went right back to my local group and haven't stopped since. The best thing that came out of this was the sharing. Several quilters told the group that they had sons or friends who died the same way and they were keeping the cause of these deaths a secret. They now felt free to come out and talk about their grief and about the person who died. They even showed pictures of panels they had made and submitted to the Names Project AIDS Memorial Quilt. It sure was a revelation to this community and it was amazing how people rose to the occasion and gave support."

Projects like the AIDS Memorial Quilt can bring communities together to memorialize those who have died. Loved ones make individual panels for the quilt that contain pictures and personal objects relating to their loved ones. The AIDS Quilt symbolizes a continuing reinvestment in life and hope. It is also a way to transform grief into direct action.

The ritual of releasing balloons has a profound effect on many who attend memorial services. Ann shared this story about her son who died of AIDS-related illness. "Ted's friends had tied regular balloons all around his coffin. In the center was a helium balloon with Ted's name on it. When the services were over, his friends released all of the balloons. As I saw the helium balloon rise higher than the others, I was able to release Ted. Before that, I couldn't even imagine how I would be able to let him go."

Other rituals can be developed such as carrying a journal to write a note when thoughts of the deceased come to mind, picking a time to listen to music that the survivor and the person who died enjoyed together, and/or holding an object belonging to the deceased while recalling a shared time.

Keep Your Sense of Humor

Humor can be one of the most successful coping skills for dealing with anger. Holding on to a sense of humor helps most everyone appreciate the lighter side of even the darkest situations. Allen Klein (no relation) in a commentary on humor and death, acknowledges that most of us believe that death is "serious business" without a place for humor [4]. Humor can, however, "provide relief for our anxieties about death by taking some of the mystery away reminding us that laughter can be beneficial." To cultivate and maintain a sense of humor, one can rent comedies, read funny books, listen to humorous stories, or visit comedy clubs. Laughter is infectious, so being with others who enjoy a funny story can also make a listener laugh.

Humor helps us cope with the death of others because it reminds us that they were more than their illness and death. As George Bernard Shaw said, "Life does not cease to be funny when people die anymore than it ceases to be serious when people laugh" [5, p. 285].

Death challenges how we see ourselves in the world. It makes us reexamine our values and explore what is truly meaningful in our life. It allows us a process of rediscovery, a look at fulfilling earlier, neglected goals, and the discovery of strengths that can take us out of the "victim" role. The energy death brings to the mourner can be used to propel him or her forward into growth opportunities previously unrecognized. Grief can be a source of inspiration.

COPING AND SURVIVAL SKILLS

- Identify stresses in life.
- Focus on soothing activities.
- Take vacations from HIV, AIDS, and death.
- Explore the arts.
- Volunteer to help those less fortunate.
- Use anger to empower, not depress.
- Pay attention to self-care, grooming, exercise, relaxation, and nutrition.
- Practice long-term survivor attributes.
- Understand that there are always choices.
- Use support systems as a forum for discussion of feelings and stresses.
- Nurture hope.
- Connect or reconnect with a religious/spiritual base.
- Develop and participate in rituals.
- Establish a new space in your life to fill with your memories of the person who died.
- Keep your sense of humor.

REFERENCES

1. S. Proffitt and B. T. Jones, On the Creative Power of Living with Death, *Los Angeles Times,* October 20, 1996.
2. D. Seabury, *The Art of Selfishness,* Simon & Shuster, Inc., New York, 1964.
3. G. Solomon, L. Temoshok, A. O'Leary, and J. Zich, An Intensive Psychoimmunological Study of Long-Surviving Persons with AIDS, *Annals of The New York Academy of Science, 496,* New York, 1989.
4. A. Klein, Commentary—Humor and Death . . . You've Got to be Kidding! in *Hospice Team Quarterly,* NHO, Arlington, Virginia, 1987.
5. Peter's Quotations, *Ideas for our Time*, Dr. Laurence J. Peter, Bantam Books, New York, 1979.

Conclusion

"Have the courage to live, anyone can die."
Robert Cody [1, p. 120]

Even though it is painful to experience the deaths of our loved ones, our life doesn't end with their deaths. We will continue to live our allotted time. Because of this, we need to be patient and gentle with ourselves, and learn to trust the process of grief. Feeling the pain of the losses is the first step toward healthy resolution. We can honor the memory of the deceased by not being afraid to feel the grief.

Most modern models of bereavement theory see grief as a working through of emotion, the eventual goal being to move on and live without the deceased. I have found, as have others in this field, that this model needs to be challenged [2]. Most mourners, with whom I have worked, want to have a safe and comfortable place to talk about the person(s) who died. They do not necessarily want to move on and let go. They also want to spend time speaking with others who knew the deceased. Contrary to popular belief, speaking of the dead does not create more sadness or grief. It allows the feelings to be freely and safely expressed. It seems that some people talk about the person who died in order to detach, while others speak of the dead in order to open a space inside them to house the feelings, thoughts, and memories of the person. Either way can be effective. The purpose of the grief experience is to help the mourner move on with, as well as without, the deceased.

Mac McCoy, a friend of mine who died of AIDS-related illness, was more than willing to share his feelings and thoughts with me on the subject of living with this disease. He was trying to reach some resolution of personal grief for his imminent death and also for his many friends who had died. "What has all this taught me?" He asked. "That life is to be lived in the now. That death is not to be feared when I truly live my life to the fullest; and that I'll be ready when it comes. That taking action helps even if I can't truly fix anything. Doing something gives me a measure of control over my own life and thoughts and feelings. Most importantly to me I have learned to better take care of myself and my needs and really enjoy life and the people in it" (Mac McCoy, personal communication, 1993).

AIDS is a serious national health problem. As we all struggle with this terrible disease and the devastation it is thrusting upon all of us, it is important to remember what has contributed to the spread of this disease. Underlying issues of inequality and injustice have been the stop signs for widespread education and prevention campaigns. It is difficult to sway public opinion on how to treat people without prejudice when they have this disease. If we are to hear the message of education and prevention as the only ways to eradicate HIV/AIDS, the stigma of being different must be erased.

Future works on AIDS grief will be focused more on populations other than the gay community. This equal opportunity virus will spread even further than it already has if people are not willing to understand that everyone is at risk of being infected. Our humanity is being given a test—to see if we can care for the sick and ease their pain and suffering without regard to race or sexual orientation. Mourners dealing with AIDS-related grief, feel pain similar to everyone elses' pain of grief. However, they struggle with multiple losses and deaths in their AIDS-affected communities dealing with discrimination as well. They need acceptance and support regardless of the cause of death.

REFERENCES

1. Peter's Quotations, *Ideas for our Time*, Dr. Laurence J. Peter, Bantam Books, New York, 1979.
2. T. Walter, A New Model of Grief: Bereavement and Biography, *Mortality, 1*:1, Carfax Publishing Co., Cambridge, Massachusetts, 1996.

Additional AIDS and General Bereavement Resources

Association for Death Education and Counseling (ADEC), 638 Prospect Avenue, Hartford, CT 06105-4250. (860) 586-7503. Fax: (860) 586-7550. E-Mail: adecoffice @aol.com. ADEC Homepage: http://www.adec.org.

Andriote, J. M. *The Special Needs of AIDS Survivors,* paper presented at the annual meeting of the Massachusetts Psychological Association, Cambridge, Massachusetts, 1987.

Brener, Anne, *Mourning and Mitzvah,* Jewish Publication Society, New York, 1993.

Colgrove, M., Bloomfield, H., and McWilliams, P., *How to Survive the Loss of a Love,* Bantam Books, New York, 1981.

Dane, B. O. and Miller, S. O., Intervening with Hidden Grievers, in *FOCUS: A Guide to AIDS Research and Counseling, 10*:1, December 1994, Auburn House, Westport, Connecticut, 1992.

Doka, K. J. with Morgan, J. D., *Death and Spirituality*, Baywood Publishing, Amityville, New York, 1993.

Fortunato, J. E., *The Spiritual Dilemma,* Harper and Row, New York, 1987.

Fuller, R., Geis, S., and Rush, J., Lovers of AIDS Victims: A Minority Group Experience, *Death Studies, 12,* pp. 1-7, 1988.

Goldstein, H. R., *Being a Blessing: 54 Ways You Can Help People Living with AIDS,* Alef Design Group, Los Angeles, California, 1994.

GriefNet, An Internet Support Community, Rivendell Resources, P.O. Box 3272, Ann Arbor, Michigan 48106-3272. (313) 761-1960. E-Mail: griefnet@rivendell.org.

James, J. and Cherry, F., *The Grief Recovery Handbook: A Step-by-Step Program for Moving Beyond Loss,* Harper and Row, New York, 1988.

Klein, S. and Fletcher, W., Care for the Caregivers, in *FOCUS: A Guide to AIDS Research and Counseling, 3*:1, December, AIDS Health Project, University of California San Francisco, 1987.

Lamm, M., *The Jewish Way in Death and Mourning,* Jonathan David Publishers, New York, 1969.

Levine, C. (ed.), A Death in the Family: Orphans of the HIV Epidemic, in *FOCUS: A Guide to AIDS Research and Counseling, 10*:1, p. 157, December 1994, United Hospital Fund of New York, 1994.

Martin, J., Psychological Consequences of AIDS-Related Bereavement among Gay Men, *Journal of Consulting and Clinical Psychology, 56,* pp. 856-862, 1988.

Names Project AIDS Memorial Quilt, 310 Townsend Street #310, San Francisco, CA 94107 (415) 863-5511.

Shilts, R., *And the Band Played On: Politics, People, and the AIDS Epidemic,* St. Martin's, New York, 1987.

Siegel, R. L. and Hoefer, D. D., Bereavement Counseling for Gay Individuals, *American Journal of Psychotherapy, 35,* pp. 517-525, 1981.

Simos, B., *A Time to Grieve: Loss as a Universal Human Experience,* Family Service Association of America, New York, 1979.

Internet Resources

GriefNet An Internet Support Community.
http://www.rivendell.org

Mental Health Net. http://www.cmhc.com/guide/grief.htm

Bereavement Research Network. http://bereavement.org/

Bereavement Resources.
http://www.funeral.net/info/brvres.html

"HIV InSite" is a World Wide Web site developed by the UCSF Center for AIDS Prevention Studies, and the AIDS Program at San Francisco General Hospital. The site offers comprehensive information about: *HIV disease and AIDS,* from prevention to clinical management, from reports on recent research data to discussions of social and ethical issues. All issues of HIV Newsline are available on the Internet at http:hivinsite.ucsf.edu. The following, from the December 1996 HIV Newsline, are web sites on the Internet that relate to HIV/AIDS that may be helpful to readers of this book:

Caregiver Resources

CDC Guide to Caring for Someone with AIDS at Home.
http://www.hivatis.org/caring.

Kairos Support For Caregivers.
http://the-part.com/kairos/.

General Resources and Information

AIDS Research Information Center (ARIC).
http://www.critpath.org/aric/.

The Body.
http://www.thebody.com/.

HIV/AIDS Treatment Information Service (ATIS) of
the U.S. Public Health Service.
http://www.hivatis.org/.
Project Inform.
http://www.projinf.org/.

ATDN's Glossary of Drugs.
http://www.aidsnyc.org/network/drugloss.html.

JAMA HIV/AIDS Library.
(Journal of the American Medical Association)
http://www.amaassn.org/special/hiv/library/libhome.htm.

Fact Sheet

National AIDS Treatment Information Project.
http://sfghaids.ucsf.edu/edulevel3factsheets.html.

Index

About the Author

Sandra Jacoby Klein, M.A., M.F.T., is in private practice in West Hollywood, California, an incorporated Creative City in the County of Los Angeles. Ms. Klein, as a psychotherapist/family therapist, specializes in the emotional effects of illness, grief, and loss. She has been working with the psychosocial issues of AIDS and AIDS grief since 1982 in her practice, and as a volunteer therapist with several AIDS service organizations in the Los Angeles area. She is a co-therapist for grief support groups, agency staff support groups, and groups for Persons Living with AIDS (PLWA). Her well-received presentations all over the world on AIDS-related grief and multiple loss syndrome are increasing understanding of the unique needs of the populations dealing with HIV/AIDS pandemic that has *affected* us all. In addition to her work as a psychotherapist and author, her creative juices flow as an enamelist. She is a founding member of Enamel Guild of Creative Arts Group San Gabriel Valley. She strongly believes in a society that can accept death as part of life and one that will support mourners through their process of grief. Ms. Klein is a long-term member and past chairperson of the Human Services Commission of the City of West Hollywood; a Clinical Member of the American Association for Marriage and Family Therapy, and the California Association of Marriage and Family Therapists; and a member of the International AIDS Society.